Dear Anna + Floyd,

Hope you enjoy!

Love,

Dorothy

Keep on the Sunny Side of Life

The Best of a Lifetime

Keep on the Sunny Side of Life

The Best of a Lifetime

By

DOROTHY M. MASTERS

A division of Squire Publishers, Inc.
4500 College Blvd.
Leawood, KS 66211
1/888/888-7696

Copyright 2000
Printed in the United States

ISBN: 1-58597-056-5

Library of Congress Catalog Card No. 00 134353

A division of Squire Publishers, Inc.
4500 College Blvd.
Leawood, KS 66211
1/888/888-7696

CONTENTS

Part I

KEEP ON THE SUNNY SIDE OF LIFE

DEDICATION

To my children, Lorna and J.B., and my beloved Loren. You made my life worthwhile!

To my family, most of you have gone on to your final resting place. Thank God for the children of Lorna and J.B. as your arrival made the departure of my birth family bearable. That is the way of life, making memories and reliving them while making new memories.

To my friends along the way, thanks for being you. Thanks for the extra love and attention.

Love,
Dorothy M. Masters

1

"NOOOOOOO-NOT another daughter!" thought Fred as Golden gave birth to Dorothy Mae Eastman. Fred, a tough, rawboned man, had six children and was trying to recover from farm and money problems created by the "Big Depression." Golden, a mild-mannered woman, smiled at her new baby as she knew the cold January weather would pass into a beautiful springtime in the Kansas Flint Hills.

She would plant garden and cook for nine people now. The year was 1936; Mom and Dad now have a "bumper crop" of kids. Little did they know that a "bumper crop" of grasshoppers were on the way! During the summer not only did the grasshoppers fly in, so did the dust. The dust storms would have been enough, but with the overabundant supply of grasshoppers, life must have been hard to endure.

I grew up hearing stories about the "dirty thirties" and how tough it was. I ate good and was always warm, so the hardships were just stories to me. I never questioned, "Who am I?" I never had to go out and "find myself!" I had been shown love and had been taken care of, so it never entered my head that I was not needed or wanted at that time in my parents' life. After all, my parents were approximately forty years of age!

I had three older brothers, Clifford, Joseph Raymond (who chose to be called Jack), Bob and three older sisters, Bessie, Elizabeth (whom we called Liz) and Helen. There were plenty of people to keep me straight with the world and to teach me the good and the bad tricks each of them had to offer.

Later, I was told by a neighbor that Bessie said when I was born, "Not another damn kid to raise!" But she babied me until the day she died and I was in my fifties. I have no complaints!

On a farm everyone has a job, and that is what you do daily! I was taught how to work at an early age, and I feel that was the best luck I ever had. It prepared me for life and how to work through the tough times ahead.

My family, for the most part, had a terrific sense of humor. I imagine being born in the thirties increased my humor, knowing I endured the bad times at someone else's expense. My family did not let the bad times decrease their overall humor. With seven kids in the family there was always someone with some fun in their head that spilled out to cause laughter even when you were not supposed to be laughing so you caught a frown from your parents.

Mother said, "Dorothy, when you were a baby, I had to put wet sheets draped over your crib to catch the dust. Wet rags were also stuffed around the windows to keep as much dust as possible out of the house!" I can only imagine how tired she grew with that extra work to protect her seventh child. It must have been hard for her and the rest of the family to retain their sense of humor until times got better!

I heard most of the tales while sitting around our round dining room table, when I was still too little to know I was poor. The oilcloth-covered round dining table was the object of my dad's humor. Dad would tell visitors, "I can never get a square meal off of this round table!" Mother was an excellent cook, and she served a square meal every time. Lord knows, she got enough practice!

We must not have been poor as our oldsters related, as our meals were always adequate. I have always been chubby, so you know I got enough to eat! But I remember vividly how hard we worked growing vegetables and fruit and milking cows so we could have good food, including beefsteak. In fact, we had pork or beefsteak for breakfast quite often. Chasing chickens and gathering eggs became one of my first responsibilities.

One evening our insurance man, Lee Bingham, stopped by to see Dad, but the folks were gone. Lee said, "Well, I will just have to stay all night so I can talk to Fred in the morning at breakfast!" Bob, my brother replied, "That's okay, Lee, but we never have any good stuff for breakfast like weenies!" Lee was from the city so it left a lasting impression on him and he mentioned it many times afterwards when we were older and he visited us.

If many mornings went by without hot biscuits for breakfast, Dad would whine, "My Mammy used to make hot bread for breakfast!"

You can bet the next morning when we came in from milking, the house smelled of hot bread baking! We had big breakfasts, but we had worked for two hours before we came to the breakfast table, so we worked up an appetite. We did many hours of work before each meal, so our appetites were good and there was no fussing about what we would eat. After working out in the country air, anything tasted good. The big problem was having enough prepared for the amount of diners.

Mom taught all of us girls how to cook as soon as we could reach the stove. I was short and can remember standing on a little chair to reach the table top and sink while learning to cook. In a large family your duties start out small and they grow as you grow. Every task was necessary to live the "good life," which we did. I had a good childhood, and my good luck has continued throughout life.

My cooking ability came in handy later when I was in school, as I cooked for the teachers and students for ball games and parties. I made big pots of chili which I sampled frequently, as I love to eat as well as cook. Which explains my title in the high school annual, "Dorothy is full of fun and jolly and when it comes to cooking, she is a hot tamale!"

I was told by my family that we were poor, and I heard my parents discussing what we could not afford. Since my belly was full and I was happy, I did not feel poor and neglected. My extra weight must have provided me a cushion against the elements of being poor. Being chubby brought me lots of attention in the form of fun and laughter. I realize a psychiatrist would say that was my reason for staying fat, but I know different. I am fat because I chose to not eat skimpy meals like anorexia people do to stay thin and eventfully die from malnourishment.

The theory at that time was fat people were jolly! I have been happy most of my life, so I guess I bought the theory and it worked for me. My late husband, Loren B. Masters, had a theory: "In every fat, jolly person there is a thin person just dying to get out!"

I love life, and eating in one form or another comes into play in every social event. I suffered the lack of genuine boyfriends for much of my life, as there is such a stigma of being fat and dating someone with extra pounds. Fitting the right poundage mold is very hard for lots of people, and the news media does not help that fact.

None of my friends in school were as chubby as I was; that did not seem to bother them much. My school mates seem to enjoy my sense of humor and my rugged physical ability, so I was one of the gang. I got plenty of exercise in the form of work and play which kept me healthy and happy. The medical community knows that moving your body with productive work or regular exercise is the best method for well being.

The only thing I could not do as a young person was to be able to wear small, pretty clothes. No one knew what a full-figured person was! My mother would buy me a blouse; I would try it on to see if it fit. I moved my arms in toward the center of my body and heard a rip! Mother would shout, "Dorothy, you ripped out the sleeve in the back!"

I would look at my mother and cry, "Well, I won't wear anything that I can't move in!" So I chose to learn how to sew my own clothes at a very young age. Then I could have well-fitting clothes in a better style. Life is a choice and we always have options. Moving, breathing deep and feeling good were always important to me.

I did not choose to follow a strict diet to be small and cute! Not to say at times I wasn't sad about being fat and would try a new approach to weight control, to no avail for any length of time. I preferred feeling good and healthy to being thin and hungry. As my friend, Marion Smith, states, "I'm mean when I am hungry!" Strict calorie reduction diets make you hungry and mean; besides, they don't work for long!

Being in the health care field, I tried the current weight control suggestions and remained fat. I have always been very physically active, so I knew that all of my body fat was not burned properly by exercise. When I entered nursing school, the Director of Nurses stated, "We will run that weight off of you in these hospital halls!"

I replied, "Don't count on it, as my dad tried that on the farm and it didn't work!" I have always walked fast since I was child, and there is a reason for my swift pace. While walking out across the corral, my dad tapped the back of my legs with baling wire that he was carrying to fix fence. I turned around and asked, "Why did you do that?" He said, "You were walking too slow!"

That kept my pace mighty swift for years to come. I am short-legged and could out-stride long-legged folks, thanks to my dad.

After marrying Loren, he would ask me, "If we go, are we going to walk or are we going on that ole nurse's trot?" I would tell him, "If you are going with me, it will be the ole nurse's trot as you call it. But to me, it is the quicken trot my daddy gave me!"

My body, in the shape it is in, has taken me along life's

path just fine, so it cannot be all bad! I knew at an early age, God made me for work, not as a small, pretty ornament to be admired! I am sure that has increased my humor as I can laugh at myself.

Many times while I was working floor duty as a registered nurse, my patients would watch me run the floor taking care of people on a "dead run." After watching my body size and my speed, they would remark, "How do you run so fast everyday and stay sooooooooo _____!" I would finish their statement, "Fat — no problem — I eat good!"

I am so grateful that my size did not cause me to develop an eating disorder such as anorexia nervosa. I often eat too much, but not to the point of inducing vomiting or excessive exercise to the point of exhaustion and death. Wanting to be thin that bad has become a very fatalistic disease in our country fueled by the news media.

I worked part-time as a school nurse after retiring from full-time floor duty and counseled many young people about proper nutrition for their growing bodies and to avoid excessive exercise without proper food and liquid replacement.

It is not unusual to see young girls worry about their size and exhibit extreme fear about "getting fat." In our country some folks do have an excessive weight problem because we have concentrated on weight in actual pounds instead being healthy and happy as the main goal.

Some of this has been caused by different sports like wrestling students, dance students and gym enthusiasts following insensible diets to fit a specific weight limit ,causing severe body and mind problems. Movie roles, standards set for models and magazines have set the trend for not liking your body as it is. Now some of the magazines are trying to turn the tables, but it will take awhile.

As parents, teachers and nurses, we need to impress the point of each and everyone being their own person, including the size and form of their body. We as role models can do a lot for our followers by accepting our own body and size.

We need to spend our time and energy on being healthy and happy. Making a good life and radiating happiness was the choice for me after I got my head on straight and stopped trying to be thin and beautiful.

Happiness is a choice and it is your responsibility — no one can make you happy!

When I was a small child, my folks' older friends would come to visit and say, "Dorothy is getting fatter every year!" (Like I wasn't in the room to hear their exclamation!) Later, the same person making the statement would say, "Here, do you want a candy bar?" — I thought, "What do you think!" As I ate the candy bar, the kind person who made the unkind remark would say, "It's just baby fat, she'll outgrow it!" At the tender age of 64, I still have my baby fat! But the joke is on them — I have fewer wrinkles! Over the years, I have developed the theory, "I am what I am!" Take me or leave me behind. The news media tries to make us think we are what we eat!

More than likely, my size and the attention I received because of it made my sense of humor greater. It cushioned me from the big jolts of life, as I do find contentment in food. I really enjoy cooking for my family and friends.

My late husband, Loren B. Masters, truly enjoyed my cooking ability, as I found out after his death. His co-workers told me after the fact that he bragged about so many of my recipes and cooking tricks. I met many of his work friends after his death as I had gone back to work at the V.A. hospital a few months before he was killed.

I felt I knew many of his co-workers and patients before meeting them just by the hospital tales Loren told me.

Many of the co-workers would ask me for a recipe that caused me to really think about the dish they were trying to describe. They always started their conversation with, "Ole Masters brought this dish to our dinner on the ward and it was so good, I want the recipe!" After some thinking on my part I could usually think of what dish they were trying to recall.

Loren and I met while working a federal hospital, and he was still working there at the time of his death. After working in the private sector for years, I returned to work in the same hospital where he worked, just six months before he was killed.

Many of the nurses and hospital staff that I met after the fact told me how Loren adored me and especially my cooking for him. I let them think they were telling me something new. That old boy, Loren, better known as "Mac" or "Short Stop," had told me that same thing one way or another for over twenty-two years. Loren would say, "Dorothy, it is about time for some roast beef salad sandwiches!" I would oblige and throw on a pot of beef to cook.

Of course, I liked good food also, so between the two of us we could dream up some heavenly delights. Our neighbor, Tony Young, would remark, "Let's have steaks on the grill tonight!" as he set down a box full of good ole Kansas Beef! We were co-dependent before the term was popular and associated with eating habits! Just in case Loren and I had not been dreaming of a different dish, Tony would come back with his culinary desires. Then the gastric juices would flow, and you can bet Dorothy got the pots and pans rattling. After a good physical workout on the farm, the three of us would salivate and plan our next feast.

We lived near Harveyville on the edge of the Kansas Flint Hills and raised cattle and pigs, so food was good and plentiful just as it had been when I was growing up.

Loren was a big, jovial man who loved his chow. He adored my cooking, and I adored him! He worked hard and I worked right by his side on the farm, as well as both of us working in the medical field, so we were both hungry at nightfall. Early into our marriage, I asked Loren if he wanted me to save some extra money by having skimpy evening meals to save on the grocery bill. He replied, "I plan to work hard every day to make money if you will plan to fix me a good supper each evening!" And that I did!

Just before his death, I looked at him and then into the mirror and said, "Mac, I think I have overdone it!" He asked, "What are you talking about?" I answered, "Do you remember when I asked you if you wanted me to save on the food bill and you discouraged me?" He said, "Yes, but tell me more!" I told him to look at me and to look into the mirror, which he did and laughed. Then I said, "Both of the deep freezes are also bulging! — I believe I have over done it!" He had a great sense of humor; he just smiled and gave me a sexy wink.

Loren was killed on his tractor while on the highway between our two farms. He was tail-ended by a car. In fact, our son, J.B., and our brother-in-law, Bill Riggin, were also on the back of the tractor but were uninjured physically. Since Loren lost his life at age forty-nine, I have regrets that I regulated any items in his diet such as eggs. He liked eggs each morning, but after the cholesterol studies I restricted eggs to two eggs twice a week for health reasons. Our bodies looked like we gorged, but we did not! We worked hard and ate good.

Loren had said often, "If I would starve enough to get thin, I would get hit by a Mac truck!" His phrase was repeated to me after his death by many friends from time to time.

The choice to work hard at raising our food is a choice I am glad we made. Loren and I taught our children, Lorna Mae and James Bryan (J.B.), to work with animals and to grow crops and vegetables just as we had been taught by our parents. Life on the farm has been good to me, and the hard work for my living has been good for my health.

Living in the country is not all work; enjoying nature along the way is an added benefit for good mental health. Happiness is so important to me; I am glad I had a happy companion for over twenty years, and his memory still brings a ray of sunshine to my life.

I sit around by myself as I watch a sunrise or sunset and just think of the remarks Loren used to make. With my memories and pictures, I still have him in my heart. Lord knows I have enough photos to refresh my mind!

Our children and grandchildren add to the joy on the farm. When the kids are here, they do a great job of bringing back very pleasant reminders of the things we did for fun with Loren. Loren had an unusual way of saying things with a flirtatious wink in his eye as we raised our kids.

2

"MOTHER, MAY I HAVE some ice in my water?" Mother replied, "No, we have to save the ice to keep the butter and milk from spoiling!" As a child, I was not allowed to have ice in my water very often but I always wished for that luxury. Mother would allow us some ice from the icebox to cool our tea in the heat of the summer but never enough to make it icy cold like I would have liked.

She had wisdom but I am sure it is hard for people in this century to understand the survival ways in the early 1900s before rural electrification. Mother had to save ice for preserving our foods as we only had an icebox. It is just as it sounds, a hunk of ice was place in one compartment and another compartment held the foods. Only the most perishable foods gained a spot in the icebox.

Some days the icebox had to be left open to retard spoilage until our parents could get to town to get another large block of ice. Some of the ice melted on the trip home and we only lived three miles from Eskridge, Kansas. But keep in mind, transportation was much different in the 1940s than it is today.

Being the youngest of seven siblings gave me no edge on luxuries. If we had extras, all of us had some not just the baby. I suppose I got the milk if supply was low which didn't happen often, I am sure. I got my chance to go out and get more milk as soon as I was able to sit on a milk stool and milk the cows.

Being able to balance yourself on a one-legged milk stool took some effort and body balance. Pulling the cow's teat with the right amount of pressure and pull was necessary to squeeze the milk in the bucket. Did I mention, you had to hold the milk bucket between your knees so the cow wouldn't kick it? It took practice and real skill to master the job so as to have enough milk for the family, plus a few squirts in the mouths of the cats now and then.

After milking, the cream was separated from the milk with a machine that was hand-operated. The animals got the extra milk, and the cream was sold in town along with the extra eggs to buy other groceries. Of course, the separator had to be washed each day and rinsed after the other milking in the evening. It took both skill and determination, as each of the discs had to be taken apart and washed individually. If you slacked on your job of washing, the folks always knew as the milk soured quicker, so they caught up with your negligence and there was Hell to pay!

My disposition became more sunny when rural electrification came to our farm about 1947 when I was eleven years old. What a luxury! Now I could have ice in my water and enough ice in the tea to make it taste like iced tea instead of cool tea. After electricity was available on the farm, I drank all the ice water that I wanted, and it is still my favorite beverage. As a nurse, I had to restrict patients by doctor's orders because of certain illnesses. As a person who loves water, and the colder the better, I pray for death instead of an illness where water is restricted for survival. Other patients you have to impress the importance of drinking plenty of water for good health.

The water was fairly cool when you drank it directly from the well, but it had to be pumped by hand and carried by the bucket to the house for general use as well as drinking, so it soon lost its coolness. I had the water-carrying detail for several years, so I was able to get cool water with each bucket, and it took lots of water to keep the family and house supplied.

The new white box was called a refrigerator, not an ice box. What a challenge for me to get used to calling it a refrigerator. To this day when I get in a hurry, I may call it the icebox! My grandchildren look at me as if I have lost my mind! If they only knew the changes I have seen in the last sixty years! That is what has stimulated me to write this legacy for them.

I enjoyed iced drinks so much I started drinking iced tea the year around, which amazed some people then. Now people drink any type of cold or hot drinks the year around because most people have good heating and air conditioning and have forgotten when we drank cool things in the summer to cool off and warm drinks in the winter to warm up.

Young people like my grandchildren were never exposed to sleeping in a room where your glass of water would freeze on the nightstand overnight and your backside would freeze while your front side was getting warm enough by the heating stove to change from your night clothes to your day attire.

Another great joy of electrification was proper lighting. It is hard to imagine now about reading by candlelight and writing all things with a pen. I never grew up with candles, as we had stinky kerosene lamps. My jobs was to fill the lamps daily with kerosene without breaking the chimneys. Each lamp made up for several candles, but it was still a challenge to read for any length of time at night.

There was no television, so reading was your best entertainment after family discussion slowed down for the evening. My dad suggested bedtime should be pretty early so we could get up and milk the cows before breakfast. His comment, "We go to bed with the chickens as we live on eggs and they will not lay anymore today!" I knew he was joking, as we had eggs for breakfast before the chickens laid more eggs.

With electricity more appliances were available for use

on the farm, but my family did not purchase many in the beginning. In time we got a family radio, not ones for individual rooms. It was such a pleasure to have some music available at your fingertips, that is to say, when Dad or Mom was not listening to the news and livestock reports. Music on the radio really brought sunshine into my life.

Another luxury was an electric iron to iron our clothes. After being used to irons that had to be heated on the cook stove that were too hot to handle and so easy to scorch the garment you were ironing, regulated heat seemed like a dream come true. Guess what? Now our clothes need very little ironing, if any, but back then all clothes were made of cotton and needed starched and ironed if you wanted to look your very best.

In time we got an electric stove for cooking but had to keep the old wood burning cook stove, as it had a reservoir to keep warm water ready for use as we did not have indoor plumbing with hot and cold water. All the water had to be heated one way or another to do dishes; there were piles of dirty dishes three times a day. Now we have dishwashers, or at least some people do, and we eat out many of our meals each week. My, have I seen some changes!

I could expound on other appliances but will not even try to explain the vast amount of technology that is in our life today; computerized cars components, for example, and all of us have many electronic gadgets, but I will mention television. It was 1950 before television came to our area but definitely not to our home before I graduated from high school and went to college. I thought I was very poor and deprived to not have access to a television at home. My first experience with TV was in the college dormitory social room.

3

"LOOK AT THE TELEVISION ANTENNA on that old shabby house! It seems to me a coat of paint would be more beneficial to that family than entertainment!" mumbled my dad as we drove along the countryside. His attitude about proper lodging versus entertainment left a solid impact on my mind. Today as I drove home from Burlingame, Kansas, I caught glimpse of a Direct Television satellite unit placed in the yard of a run-down ramble shack. I immediately thought of my dad and what he said during my childhood when television was new.

I bought my dad's sense of worth and the need for necessities over the lust for enjoyment and luxuries. I guess that theory is where the saying, "The apple does not fall far from the tree!" was originated! However, I raised a couple of "apples" that do not always share in my belief or Dad's theory.

When I was a child, I too wanted a television after it was invented and perfected and came to our area. But my dad did not buy one, as he knew food and necessities absorbed most of the money available. Also, he knew the time used to watch T.V. was needed to do necessary farm chores. My dad died before he was able to justify buying a set, and we lived without one.

Today I swallow hard when I hear a young bread winner list their luxury appliances and talk about his or her paycheck not stretching far enough to pay for utilities and groceries.

After high school, I entered nurses' training and gained luxuries like indoor plumbing in the living quarters. Yes, there was a T.V. set on each floor of the nurse's dormitory in the social room but not in individual rooms.

At last I gained access to entertainment with the twist of a knob. But time was a problem. I had to work at the hospital for eight hours a day, attend class for four hours, sleep, eat, do my home work, clean my room and launder my clothes. I could then watch all the T.V. I wanted to until 10:30 p.m. when lights were to go off. Needless to say, I did not get addicted to television, but I had a chance to watch it occasionally. What a treat!

When and if my grandchildren read this, it will be hard for them to relate. It is easy to take for granted what has always been available for your use.

One time when J.B. was in college, he was with me in the grocery store and he thought I was buying too much. He made the statement, "If you were in college, you would learn to do without!" I replied, "I was in college and I did without and I did not have a T.V. or a truck!" He shrugged his shoulder and mumbled, "Oh, geez!" He knew immediately he had spoken out of turn!

Loren told a different story about he and his family getting electricity and television. His dad, Bryan Masters, bought a fifth of whiskey and bribed my brother, Jack Eastman, who worked for the Eskridge Kansas Power and Light, to hook up their farm to electricity earlier that the planned date. Knowing both of those fellows, I can easily believe that tale. Dad Masters wanted to catch a ball game that was being televised!

Back to my enjoyment of modern conveniences, I lived in the country before nursing and had good natural air ventilation. When I left for the city to go to school, my sister, Bessie Eastman, gave me a big fan as she knew this warm body would be miserable in the city without good air circulation.

I felt like a Queen to have my own fan and radio. I forgot who gave me the radio, but I sure enjoyed both. I do not recall how many students had radios, but I was the only one with a fan. It was not uncommon to come back to my room and find someone stretched across my bed cooling in front of the fan.

I was in school before they had air conditioning in the hospital in Kansas City. That is hard to believe now. But you now understand how a fan and a radio could bring so much sunshine into my life.

4

WHEN I WAS A CHILD, the talk about the man in the moon was fairytale talk. But I lived to see a man walk on the moon! The fairytales said the moon was made of green cheese, but the astronauts found it to be made of rocks, just like our wonderful Flint Hills.

At that time Loren and Tony Young baled lots of prairie hay and alfalfa. Loren said to Tony, "You and I can get the first hay baling contract on the moon!" I protested as I was their "loader man" when I was away from hospital duty. I put bales on the elevator which carried them up and into the barn. I said, "I need both feet on the ground to lift those bales, and I could see when Neil Armstrong walked on the moon, he was floating in air!" They both laughed, and that was the last discussion about haying jobs on the moon.

I know very little about the discovery on the "moon walk," but I remember watching the news on television and it was very impressive to me at the time. Seeing fairytales come true was fascinating. I have seen so many changes in transportation that I am unable to remember all the details, and that is why we have reference books and libraries.

I am recording my memories for my children and grandchildren, but they will have to research the details because each change in transportation takes many books to explain all of the aspects.

I remember well the first motorized vehicle the my dad bought after I was big enough. He bought a 1947 Dodge pickup. I can still remember how proud we were to be riding in that new truck.

There is a whale of a difference in riding in a pickup instead of on the back of a horse. I grew up riding a horse, and that seemed like good transportation at the time. It sure beat walking across the pasture to get the cows or work horses.

I was the "water boy," so the horses, "Brownie" or "Dan,' were kind enough to carry me and the water jug to each man working in our fields. The number of workers changed depending on the time of the year and who was working for Dad.

In the early 1940s the German prisoners were living in a camp at Lake Wabaunsee. The local farmers could employ them as farm workers. I was too little to remember lots of details, but I vividly remember the guard's dog, which was a German Shepherd, that bit brother, Bob Eastman, on the thigh. I remember Bob's reaction, and he was scared of big dogs after that, especially German Shepherds. His comment after the fact, "That damn dog was supposed to bite the Germans, not me!"

I do remember that it was not my job alone to deliver water to the fields at that period of time. Mother had to go to the field and furnish a snack to the German prisoners as well as water, so I imagine we went by horse and wagon in order to haul the food. But the rest of the water trips were left to me and my horse when it was just my dad, brothers and "regular" hired men in the fields.

My dad was happy to see me and the water jug, but he frowned when he saw me climb the fence to get back on my horse after opening and closing the gates. I was too short and chubby to jump on the horse, not enough spring in my short, fat legs. I could have put on the saddle but bareback was easy, and I liked to ride bareback. However, Mother did not like the way the horse's sweat stained my clothes.

Most of my fond memories are when I think what I did

in the country with my family, especially when a horse was involved. During my early childhood I was taught how to ride a horse both for fun and to do the chores. Cliff and Bob were real horsemen. Bob could handle a horse and ride like a real wrangler.

My favorite brother, Bob, was three years older than I, and if he was not working in the field, we were playing with the horses. He was an excellent horseman, and he did his best to make me a good cowgirl. He had more riding talent than I did, and he was much more brave and daring on a horse. Usually we rode bareback, which was just fine for Bob, but I could not jump on like he could. I would find a barrel, fence post with sturdy wire stapled tightly or some object to put extra spring in my step. My dad was not happy when he saw me use the fence and caused the staples to fly out of the posts. With my weight I could cause those staples to really fly through the air. Dad seemed to smile more when I took time to saddle the horse, as he knew there would be a gate in my path before my ride was completed.

I acted tough at times, but inside I would be so scared that I might get hurt and suffer the consequences. I had suffered the consequences more than once after escapades with Bob and the horses. Dad let his work team out to pasture every night. Bob was supposed to ride a saddle horse out to get the team immediately after breakfast. I was supposed to stay in the barn yard so Bob wouldn't play along the way and get the job done so Dad could get to the field. When Dad was out of sight, I jumped on behind Bob and we were off on a dead run to the pasture to get the horses. Maybe we could get back before Dad missed me in the barnyard. Bob like to ride like the wind, and I would hang on for dear life!

Besides riding fast, Bob's next passion was making the horse jump ditches, and that scared me silly. On our early morning run to bring in the team, Bob tried to get "ole Dan" to jump the ditch, but Dan decided to shy and walk through.

I lost my balance and started to fall off, so I pulled Bob off with me.

We got back to the barn with wet jeans, so Dad tapped our back sides as he knew we had been together playing, which delayed his trip to the field.

My dad meant business when he spoke so I do not know why we pushed him, but we did all for the sake of having fun. I just loved to be out with Bob, even if it cost me a whipping in wet jeans now and then.

Another time I thought I was in trouble for riding my horse when Dad scolded me for running the horse across the Flint Hills in the big pasture we rented from Bill Hentzler. The pasture was on fire and we had not set it. In front of the firemen, my dad said, "Dorothy, it is your fault for running the horse across these flint rocks the other day!" The firemen laughed, and I figured out he was teasing me for a good laugh.

My dad was a fun-loving man, but when he had work to do he was dead serious. With a family of nine mouths to feed, working for a living was serious!

Once in awhile, I wondered if I would survive while playing with Bob, as he tried to make me tough enough to survive without him. When he hurt me accidentally from being too tough, he would love me, thus preventing me from telling Mother. He was older and wiser about covering his tracks where the folks were concerned

Dad liked to have all of his mules and team horses broke to ride bareback so he could jump a straddle one of them and ride to the house and leave his implement in the field at night.

To break the mules or work horses, Dad would ride one of the saddle horses and snub a mule to the saddle horn, then lead the animal to be broken along side of the hayrack, and Bob would jump on its back and break him to ride.

One Sunday when there was a nice covering of snow on the ground, Dad decided to break a mule to ride. I always got a safe place to watch the action, which usually turned into a rodeo of sorts. As soon as Bob was astride the mule, he would yell, "Now I'm on!" In a matter of seconds the mule pitched Bob off, and Dad would yell, "Now you're off!" That scene was repeated several times before the mule gave in and let Bob ride him for any distance.

My dad was a horse trader as well as a mule skinner. He would bring some strange-looking animals into our yard that would quite often wipe the grin off my mother's face. Mother was a serious-minded woman, and her reason for being so was simple to me. She had to keep her nose to the grindstone to keep us all fed and clothed. I could tell she would see dollar signs when she first saw Dad's animals that he had traded for and was planning to make money on, with Mother's reservations. Some of them were sorry-looking critters! But in spite of Mother's fears, Dad fattened up the critters and usually made some money.

One of the best riding horses we had when I was a kid looked like a bag of bones when Dad brought him home. Mother nearly fainted when she saw that skinny horse, and she exclaimed, "Fred, that horse is going to die!" But Brownie lived! My dad gave that horse some good care, and Brownie provided us with lots of work and fun times for years. I guess, "You can't judge a book by the cover!" Sometimes dumb luck is better that skilled planning.

The best thing that Mother pulled in the way of humor was about Dad and his mules. When she heard a commotion in the barn as Dad was getting his mules harnessed to go to work, Mother said, "Your dad will never have a heart attack because he doesn't have a heart!" Dad had the opinion that to work mules, you must first get their attention, and that is what all the noise was about!

My brother, Cliff, was a nervous type individual, and he had a son, Charley, who appeared real easy-going. Charley would get out of the truck to open the pasture gate; he would look up and down the fence as if he was lining it up. Cliff would honk the horn , grasp the steering wheel and snort, but he never hurried up Charley. Guess what? Charley never slowed Cliff down, but it was quite a sight to see. I was six years older than Charley, and I wondered how Charley could get by with pestering his dad, as my dad would have done more than honk and snort!

When Bob and I were growing up, we spent a lot of time at Cliff's farm with him and his wife, Mildred. We really liked Mildred's good cooking; she spoiled us. Cliff was a good stockman and farmer and was no slouch on a horse. Bob was a real horseman, and since Charley and I were younger we were impressed with Bob's ability.

One day Bob was riding one of Cliff's quarter horses and getting a great performance out of the horse. Cliff said in amazement, "Bob, you can do better with him than I do. Why?" Charley piped up, "Well, Dad, you sit up on him like a sack of shit!" No more questions were asked. Cliff shook his head and walked off to leave Bob and Charley snickering.

We had lots of amateur rodeos at our family farms over the years. Bob was a fool-kid, trick rider, and we encouraged him to do more as we enjoyed his antics. Charley improved with age, but Bob usually got me into tricks over my head and God-given abilities. I lived through it, but at times I wondered, now I know the answer — God is not through with me yet!

Bob liked rough riding, and he took many hard falls in spite of my mother's fear of him getting hurt. He did many tricks from his horse; in fact, he was the one who taught me to pull him off at just the right time. Lord only knows, he did it enough times.

One day on top of our big black horse, Dan, Bob had him running fast as we came over a big hill. Bob slid off, pulling me with him, and together we rolled down the hill as the Dan went it alone. Bob thought it was fun, and I thought it was dangerous as I stopped laughing. However, I kept riding with him bareback on the horses. One might think I was a glutton for punishment! I was happy to be out with Bob playing in spite of the risks involved.

He was a good cowboy and a heck of a horseman, but he never held it against me because I was not a terrific cowgirl. But I could hold my own and ride for pleasure and chores, but the tricks were left up to Bob most of the time.

Tricks on horses planned by Bob and mostly done by Bob were the only real entertainment that I remember as a child, but looking back there is nothing to compare for the money it cost. It was not only horses and mules that provided my entertainment. Bob also rode calves. The neighbor boys rode with him. One way or another, I would end up the guinea pig, and how they enjoyed the entertainment at my expense! Two of our neighbors, Jack Peoples and Bob Kraus who were kids at the time, have to remind me of the times they talked me into going up the ladder into the hayloft because they said, "Ladies first!" It took me awhile to figure out why they wouldn't let me jump down first!!!! It makes for great conversation in our old age.

Bob and I grew up in spite of our fun and games; we survived our childhood capers. We made our own fun, no matter what, and that seems to be a lost art today.

5

SEX EDUCATION: at an early age, it was not on the farm agenda. Believe me, you learned by accident or not at all. Dad was talking to a man out in the corral when I noticed a bull mounting a cow, I yelled, "Dad, that bull is going to kill that cow!" Bob knocked me off of my perch up on the top of the gate. I got up and asked, "Why did you do that?" He replied, "To get your mind on different things!" It did that!

The folks told me that the neighbor lady, Mrs. Tucker, just brought her milk cow down to visit our bull yearly. I said, "That is dumb!" No one bothered to explain the facts of life to me. Later, I figured it out little by little.

When I look back at some of my experiences before and after marriage, it is a wonder I lived to enjoy old age. I was 57 when I retired from active nursing and no wonder I felt 75 on some days. My family had a strange way of teaching breeding procedures so I could figure out sex and what it was all about.

I was so dumb when I began nursing school, I am sure my mouth dropped open more than once at the sight of birthing and terms of sexual practices. My personal instructions were, "You will need these pads once a month; keep yourself clean and smelling good as "fat people" stink more. Don't mess with boys!"

I knew my children would be taught from an early age as to breeding procedures and sexual practices. When J.B. was just a little tad, he shocked my mother!

Loren taught all of us to report to him if we observed

any cow being bred so he could keep records. My mother was riding in the truck out in the pasture with us and J.B. announced to his dad that, "Dad, the bull bred 'Dolly' yesterday!" My mother gasped for air, and I know she thought, "What is this world coming to!" as J.B. was so small he was standing up behind his dad's shoulders.

Lorna and J.B. continued their education of breeding procedures and the birthing routine when our bird dog had puppies. When I took the children up to see the puppies, she had two more. J.B. was just a toddler, and as he walked down from the barn with his little hands behind his back, he remarked, "How about that — they came right out her butt!"

That night, Lorna explained the entire procedure to her dad at the supper table. During the discussion, we answered their questions and cautioned them it was a subject for family talk only. The next day, J.B. shared it with his second family — the baby sitter's little 18-month-old baby. Laura, the baby sitter, overheard the entire explanation and thought it was a scream.

The next time J.B. spoke of animal breeding procedures, he really surprised an older friend of mine. She was not a farmer and never lived on a farm. J.B. asked Harriet, "Did you ever hear of a bull breeding a cow through a fence." She asked me later, so I explained that was what Loren had asked Glen the night before. The question was never answered, but we had a calf that was not our breed so something funny had taken place in our pasture.

J.B. now has his own herd of cattle, so I guess it is a good thing he did as much research as possible when his dad was alive to help him with the answers.

I am very pleased that Loren and I decided to teach our children about sexual animal practices and humor behavior in a different manner than which I was taught, or should I say the manner in which I was not taught. Ignorance is not always BLISS.

GOLDEN, MY MOTHER, said, "Scrub your body good, as you are fat and you will stink if you don't!" as she showed me by scrubbing her own creases and fat roll! During my childhood I learned some valuable lessons that I think of quite often as I get older. When I sit close to a chubby person and can smell their body odor, I appreciate my mother's advice.

She told me and showed me the best way she knew how. Mother did not have an education past sixth grade, but she got her point across. I remembered the lesson and still value it today.

Mother's clean ways helped me through life; I had a head start on cleanliness when I started nurse's training. I used the technique when bathing patients and kept them smelling like a rose. In fact, I still use it today as I do one home health patient and, my, how she hates to take a bath. When people get older they hate water — they hate to drink or wear it!

When I started nurse's training, lots of my earlier education took meaning. I was only eighteen, and all of the things I learned at home were foremost in my mind.

I had been taught at home that we were "poor," as my parents mentioned it when some unneeded articles were spoken of, like indoor plumbing and a TV. When I reached college, I found out from my roommates what it was like to grow up without the necessities such as proper food and adequate love! Hearing the young ladies in our dormitory talk about not having enough food or love left an impression on me. It made me feel well loved and appreciate my heritage.

When I would hear the term "dumb farmer," I would be fuming. More than one time I replied to that phrase, "They are smart enough to grow all of the food you eat!"

It was during that period of my life that I learned to appreciate my farm heritage and fully understand that one is not "poor" if they have food and love!

Also, during that experience I figured out that a person has to learn at an early age to work and provide for their own welfare, and that includes happiness. This makes for a happy and healthy lifestyle. I feel one must be happy to radiate sun to others' lives and to make a good life for yourself. Happiness is your responsibility!

I was quickly aware that not everyone in this world was happy and secure. Good senses of humor do not just happen; security is the first requirement. You must feel secure and feel good about yourself! Security comes from within; then the sun shines into your life. Sharing your sun makes you have a bigger glow!

I am sure that my arrival in 1936 with the grasshoppers must have warped my folks' humor for awhile, since they had not fully recovered from the Depression and the bank failures. But I tried to make them laugh as soon as I was able to coo and crack jokes. My older siblings taught me how to tell jokes and provide laughter for others.

I WANTED AN EDUCATION for as long as I can remember, and I still want to learn something new each day. Only now I have more trouble with the retention of information, but that goes with the territory, the natural aging process.

Many of my friends hate to hear me say, the normal aging process! But I am an honest person and I tell it like it is. I also buy the theory, "What you don't use — you will lose!"

Only now, I can't move and use as much daily as I once did and, believe me, I am losing more ability that I like. Lord only knows what would happen if I did not give it my full effort!

I had very good role models as a small child and still know people today in the educational field that I admire. I had some great teachers when I was young; in fact ,my fifth grade teacher, Mrs. Maxine Daily, left an impression for life. She was rigid and strict, but she helped me in every way. I was used to rigid and strict as my parents were just that. There was no nonsense when they give instructions, and I followed their wishes to the letter. Mrs. Daily was knowledgeable, lovable and a very caring person. She comes to mind quite often as I first wrote this book. In fact, she offered to help me in any way that she could. She already helped me with her basic, sound education! Since the first writing she has died and will not see the finished project ,but her memory is very much a part of my book.

I learned from watching the behavior of my older

brother, Jack, and sister, Elizabeth. It was easier to listen to my dad than to take the consequences, because there was Hell to pay when they disobeyed.

Besides a couple of non-conforming people in our family, I observed kids in schools who were unable to accept the rules. By today's society, they would be labeled Attention Deficit Disorder, but we just called them trouble makers. They paid the price! From the beginning, it appeared easier to me to follow the rules and I am glad that I did — good decision!

Three high school teachers stand out in my mind as excellent teachers. Mr. Olin Church was our principal; he was mild-mannered, but he meant business and you knew it. Mrs. Mary Carrington was my Home Economics teacher, and she lives only a few miles away from my country home. We show up at many of the same activities. She still sews daily and shares her talent of cooking. Mary, as I call her now days; it took me forever to be able to call her Mary, but she insisted many times that I drop the Mrs. since we both have aged! Mary still builds up my character by what she says to me and about me to others. We quite often show up at the same luncheon.

When I think of my success in life because of educational opportunities, my mind leads me to the memory of Miss Murrel Dill, my English teacher. I wish I could call her about sentence structure and punctuation when I get in a bind. But God called her home several years before I started hobby writing. I get great satisfaction in knowing she is correcting my book from above. Unfortunately, I am sure I am missing lots of her clues. When I get in a tight spot, I can close my eyes and see her stomp her foot to get my attention. She wore the black-laced shoes with cuban heels, and she knew how to get the class' attention by clicking her heels or stomping her foot.

Lots of my classmates were not as fond of her as I was at the time, but I hear nothing but respect from them now!

Many of my friends have remarked later in life about missing the opportunity of utilizing her wisdom.

Miss Dill brought lots of sunshine into my life and encouraged me to use my God-given talent in passing my sunshine to others. She helped me to realize my sense of humor and how I could use it to brighten others' lives. Many of my patients over the years have been grateful for her teaching ability.

I am so lucky to have so many friends and so many good memories of friends that are no longer in my social circle.

Before my formal years of education, my role models were also good, my parents and older siblings. My parents taught me honesty and integrity. They provided the structure in which I could learn to work and live as a good human being. Being born into a rural, hard-working family was the best luck I ever had. By example, my parents were the best teachers I ever had.

Loren was the next best teacher; he taught me many different ways to work on the farm and earn my own place in the world. I adore all of my dear teachers in the past, and I still look for a positive teacher today.

I HAVE ALWAYS BEEN an independent cuss. The year I was fifteen I had a horrible Christmas, as my teeth were so rotten that I was unable to eat sweets because of toothaches. Back then, we always had the majority of our sweet foods for our Christmas holidays. I couldn't eat them, so it made for the worst Christmas I have ever had.

After Christmas I drove Mother to the store and left her there to shop while I went to the dentist. Mother never drove the car after I was big enough, so I drove her wherever she needed to go.

While I was at Dr. Pratt's office, I asked him, "Can you pull my teeth out between now and when school is out? Can you make me dentures and have them fitted before I go back to school in the fall?"

Dr. Pratt agreed and pulled ten teeth instead, only the teeth that were bothering me. All of my teeth had been filled and were rotting more.

I had made arrangements to pay him for the dentures the following summer when I could work out and make some money. He agreed with no questions asked!

When I got downtown to pick up Mother, I was missing ten teeth, and she nearly had a heart attack! Her first words were, "How are we going to pay for your dentures?"

I answered, "No problem — he will carry me on the books until next summer, and I will work out to make the money!"

I did just that! I lived with my sister, Bessie, who lived

and worked in Topeka. I got a job right after school for the summer doing waitress work at the Purple Cow, which was the coffee shop in the Hotel Kansan.

After high school I was eager to get out into the real world to make a living for myself and for my family, should the need ever arise. When my husband was killed before my children were grown and educated, I knew why the good Lord had steered me towards nurse's training.

While in grade school, I noticed the students from the Catholic school at Newbury got the blue ribbons in spelling and math while I had to settle for the red ribbons. That made me pick a Catholic school. The only thing I knew about a Catholic education was their strict structure and discipline. They had to have discipline in order to always get the blue ribbons!

After taking the pre-examination and passing, I was off to get my entrance physical. The physician did not like my extra weight, so he did not pass me for the nursing school. Believe me, he was not the first person to hate my extra fat.

I was in a panic when I left his office but headed back to St. Francis Hospital to face the nun. Thank God, she was fat and knew not to judge a book by its cover.

She grabbed my entrance physical form and started writing on the form where the doctor had stated he would advise the school to deny me entrance. She wrote, "Accepted!" She looked at me and smiled, and said, "He doesn't know a thing about being fat!" Thank God the Nun was chubby and knew about weight problems.

When I left the hospital, I was as happy as I was sad when I left the doctor's office. That nun really knew how to put sunshine in my life.

My extra fat had kept me from lots of things like pretty clothes, dates and some sports, but I was accepted into the school of my choice, so I knew this body in the large mold would take me most of the places that I really wanted to go if I had the perseverance.

Believe me, it took perseverance to stick with nurse's training in the fifties. We worked on the floors as a student nurses eight hours each day, then we had four hours of class. We did not have the summers, weekends and holidays off because we were students and manned the hospital so regular staff could be off except for the supervisor.

When we were seniors, the Federal Government passed a law for forty hours a week. By the time the law was passed and enforced, most of our classes were over and we were studying for our state boards. So the last few months of our three-year period, we only worked forty hours a week. We thought we were on vacation or died and gone to Heaven.

Vacations while in school were few and far between, which is a big change from college classes today. As I was informed by a nurse older than I was at the time, we were trained as a nurse to work as a nurse; today nurses are educated — Big Difference. I mulled that statement over in my mind; she said a very profound statement as I thought about the words!

We were trained to do work after a comprehensive course at college, but most of our education was from practical experience with a registered nurse watching over us. In fact, one of my supervisors would follow me so close when I was passing medications that my breathing was impaired, but she did not allow me to make any errors.

Today's registered nurses have very little practical experience when they hit the job market, but they can write a "pretty" story about the patient on the chart. We were trained to do the nursing care and to document in short profound phrases when the care was completed. When excessive documentation became a rule, it was hard for trained nurses to sit and write so much, especially when there were more nursing tasks to be done. This being a fact, the years just before retirement were difficult for old trained nurses like me. Some of the care is compromised when excessive charting is required, making my hospital experience impossible for me toward the end.

I am grateful for the structure and discipline that was provided by the Catholic nuns as they trained me to take my nursing responsibility very serious. But I must say they also scared the "pants" off of me on several occasions.

We were instructed to say, "Yes, Sister" or "No, Sister!" One cold day my bedroom was cold, so I went down to the office to say that the radiator must be broken as it was cold in my room. Sister took one look at me and said, "You probably broke it!" And I said, "Yes, Sister," and left the office. I didn't freeze to death as I lived to tell the story! I knew I was big and I had been told I was bad at times but me — break a steel radiator!

The nuns surprised me at other times, but for the most part they added sunshine to my life and taught me how to capture my own sunshine.

We had a lot of fun as well as steady work. One nun taught me how to do the polka. They knew how to enjoy themselves, but when you were on the job they taught you how to work and be professional.

This little "ole country gal" had some trouble leaving the farm behind and being in the city. When we were taught how to take temperatures and to shake down the thermometers, a remark I made followed me the rest of the time in nurse's training. I was trying to learn how to shake down thermometer without letting hit against a hard object or slip out of my hand. After some struggle, I said, "I can milk a cow quicker than I can shake down a thermometer!" My classmates ran that expression past me many times when they saw me struggle to shake down a thermometer.

Before I finished my career, we took patients' temperature in their ear. I worked at a veteran's hospital when the ear thermometers came on the market, and the patients marveled when I stuck the device into their ear. I would laugh as I said, "I always wanted to tell you fellows to stick it in your ears and now I do it myself!" No more shaking down thermometers, just change the batteries!

My mouth has gotten me in trouble many times, but one time I recall the nuns had me stay in bed and miss a day's work to rest my voice so I could talk that night at the party. The nuns were having an appreciation dinner for the staff doctors and we students were doing the entertainment. I was planning to give my high school reading, "The Reducer." Since I was fat and the doctors were always on my case, the nuns sure wanted me to recite my reading, which was a clever rendition about how large people rationalize each morsel of food that we put into our mouths.

I enjoyed the day in bed to rest my throat and to let my laryngitis clear up, but I was amused when I would think that my family did not let me miss chores so I could talk longer or better! Usually my family wanted me to "shut up," and they told me that I talked so much that I made their ears bleed.

I do love to talk and I guess that is why I am writing this book. I still have so much to say, and I live alone and no one to talk to most of the time. When people come, I talk so fast in order to get it all said before they leave. I do notice now and then their ears are bleeding. I call the excessive fast talking the "Widow Syndrome!"

I find this way to be the best to share my experiences with my children and their children. I wanted to share my sunshine with others and decided this would be the best method. I used to share my sunshine with my patients but have become too old to run the hospital halls every day.

I am just like Dolly Parton, I have come "Full Circle!" I started my career by answering call bells to care for patients and ended my career by being called by the computer to accept a substitute school nursing position at one of the schools in Topeka. I worked as a school nurse on a part-time basis for several years after quitting full-time floor duty in a hospital. The computer would call me in the morning, and I would push buttons as to whether or not I would accept the position at the school.

I did not accept any jobs unless I felt like working that day. I had no guilt feelings, as I think after forty years in a career one should have a "cushy" job or no job at all!

After I quit taking the school jobs, sometimes I would feel lazy in the mornings, but as I told J.B., "I roll over and go back to sleep and the feeling goes away!"

Making money and having a satisfying career were only two of the assets of my nursing career; developing lifetime friends has been the real enjoyment of my life.

ONE OF MY BEST FRIENDS, Carol Weekes, became my friend when we entered the grade school in Eskridge in the fourth grade. Both of us had attended separate country grade school for the first three grades. Town school was a big change for both of us. Carol was a shy, scared little rabbit, and I missed playing on the playground almost at will. I had been the only student in my grade at the country school, and as soon as I got my work done, I could go out and play!

I guess we formed a close knit friendship to hold our own against the town kids and all of the new surroundings. For whatever the reason, I am grateful as we are still close friends today. Although she lives in California, tapes, letters and phone calls keep us connected.

We both worked at the Purple Cow, which was a coffee shop in the Hotel Kansan in Topeka for the summer between our senior year of high school and college. I had worked there the previous summer and lived with my sister, Bessie. Carol stayed with me at Bessie's apartment. There was a screened back porch just behind Bessie's apartment, so I slept out there with Carol.

As Carol would say, "We had a bad night on the porch!" Sometimes when lightning would flash and the thunder would rock our beds, Bessie would take pity on us and let us crawl in bed with her. Then Bessie had a bad night sharing her bed with us!

Our friendship grew, and we were maids of honor for

each other's wedding. We shared many memorable moments together and never needed much in the way of entertainment, as we could sit on the curb and have plenty of good laughs together.

Carol followed her husband, Stan Swenson, around the states while he was in the Air Force, and he retired from the service when they lived in California. They remained there, but we have always kept in touch. Our different lives for a lot of years prevented us from visiting one and another in person, but now our relationship is closer and tighter than ever.

When I became a widow, she became my number one confidant. Stan was so good to talk with me about things; I needed to hear a man's opinion. The three of us had many vacations together over the years before his death. Then Carol and I had to go it alone, and we went together many places. Now each of us is happy to stay at home and enjoy our grandchildren when possible.

Carol is the type of friend that I can tell anything to and she will try to understand. She will give me her honest opinion even if it doesn't agree with my thinking. That is what makes her so priceless as a friend and a close confidant!

We tape our thoughts back and forth most of the time. This makes the answers delayed, but at least I get answers. Then I fire back a rebuttal. When Stan was alive, he would give his opinion and then we could really rap about the subject.

It is so wonderful to have a close friend and have them for a lifetime. We can sit on the street corner, laugh and giggle and have the best time. In fact, we giggle a lot. We find things to laugh about, and people look at us as if to say, "What's so funny?"

On one of our vacations I flew to their home in Sacramento, California, and then Stan drove us to Tijuana, Mexico. When he left us to do our own thing, he reminded us, " Girls, this is not Eskridge!" That told us we were out where our giggling could lead us to big trouble.

Stan never put a damper on our fun; he liked to keep us safe. He knew we would find fun on our own. To tell the truth, he enjoyed seeing us have so much fun just being together.

I have had lots of friends over the years, but never anyone that I enjoyed more or who knew me so well. By mentioning just one word, we can stir up laughter from the other one about a subject that gave pleasure many years ago. Many times I would call Carol, and Stan would answer and say, "How did you know Carol needed to talk to you?" I had the reply, "I needed to talk to her!"

This book will never end if I mention all of the friends that help to light up my life. But I must mention Mary Lou Riat, as I met her in nurse's training and we have been very good friends. After I was married, she married Herb Anderson.

Mary Lou is a wonderful cook, and she would spoil Loren and me with our favorite dishes when she felt we needed some extra T.L.C. She would make Loren a pecan pie and me a lemon cake. We entertained each other's family for all those years, and what great fun we had. Of course, food always was a part of the good times; we loved to eat! Cooking used to be one of my skills, but I have lost some skill due to lack of practice.

My classmates in high school put the caption, "Dorothy is full of fun and jolly; when it comes to cooking, she's a hot tamale!" under my picture in the yearbook.

I guess I deserved the caption while in high school, as I made chili for the school events on many occasions. In fact, I made much more than chili.

When you live with a large family, you learn how to cook early in life. I have always been fat and love to eat even my own cooking! I have always told my friends when they compliment my cooking ability, "One doesn't get this big without learning to cook your own food!"

I have cooked for large numbers of people over the years and truly enjoyed the extra work. The gratification was outstanding! Our friends, Bob and Gladys Slade, always had a big fish fry in July for Bob's birthday. Bob would start fishing in early spring by setting lines, and by July he had more than enough for over one hundred people. I started helping them fry the fish in electric skillets in Gladys' kitchen until I burned plugs off skillets, I would fry so long! To say nothing of a very messy kitchen floor!

I never changed my recipe for coating the fish, but the equipment changed greatly over the years. In time, I inherited the entire frying job, but I had equipment that handled the job.

We had a outdoor grill made to grill meat and a rack for a large frying skillet to use for deep fat frying. Tony Young went by the shop where the grill was been built and ordered a stand for it so it would be portable. It was big enough for two pans (military surplus) to sit on top, and that is how I got the entire fish-frying detail! Then it seems like Bob caught more fish, but I fried outside and let the grease fly.

Many of those friends and Loren have gone on to get their rewards in Heaven. So I rarely do that kind of cooking any more but have never forgotten the fun and the praise that I had while it lasted. The memories and pictures will stay in my mind forever ...

When Loren was alive and running cows and calves on pasture, we ate real good. Stan and Carol Swenson would come back from California, and we would throw steaks on the grill and sit down to chew the fat! Stan always remarked about the "good ole Kansas Beef!" Later, when I went to states like Arizona, New Mexico and California and saw the grazing of cattle, I could sure notice the difference in the pasture land; it was definitely not the Kansas Flint Hills!

My friend, Joy Hill, gave me a plaque that reads, "The best antiques are old friends." I think that tells it all!

Bette Watson was my best friend during my nursing

career. I met Bette when I first graduated and went to work at a veteran's psychiatric hospital. She was a seasoned nurse, so she took me under her wing at work. We did many social events together. She and her husband, Randy, had a small boy, Mike, at the time, so I doubled as a baby sitter sometimes. With Bette's help and friendship, I became a very secure registered nurse. Boy, does it help when a friend takes you under their wing until you get your feet solidly on the ground. In nursing you have to dig your toe in and hang on like HELL if you want to survive your career! Today, there is a word for that — mentor. Bette was my mentor before I knew about the word!

My family was very supportive to me and my career. Nursing is shift-work, weekends and most holidays, so a cooperative family is a must if you survive your career and raise children.

10

MY FAMILY HAS always been important to me, and being from a large family made it better. I was fortunate to have started out in a large family, but death came to my father when I was only nineteen, and my mother died when I was in my early forties. The losses due to death have taken a toll, and I only have one sister, Elizabeth (better know as Liz to me), left at the time of this writing.

When my father was dying of cancer, I was away at college in Leavenworth at St. Mary's College for girls. That college was run by the Sisters of Charity as were St. Francis Hospital in Topeka and Providence Hospital in Kansas City, Kansas. My father was becoming more gravely ill and I was so far from home. I longed to be back in Topeka at the hospital where I could see my family more often. I had planned to return to Topeka and complete my training where I had enrolled, but there was a big surprise!

A few days before our return to Topeka, our class was told we would have to complete nurses' training at Providence in K.C. The school of nursing was being closed in Topeka, as their student housing was condemned by the city.

I was devastated, my father was dying and I had to go further away from home to finish my schooling! I am big on completing what I start, and my college credits would not transfer to the nursing school at Stormont in Topeka. So I swallowed hard and went to K.C. with the class. Therefore,

I graduated from Sisters of Charity School of Nursing at Providence Hospital in Kansas City, Kansas.

Dad died before long after I was transferred to K.C., and his death was harder on me than if I had been able to spend a few more hours with him from time to time. Remember, transportation was not as it is today. I had to ride the bus to and from K.C., which took considerably longer.

I feel that was an extra loss during my life that I was not planning. After enduring many losses, one had to find a way to let the sun shine upon you, to reap all its warmth. I have plenty of sun, as I was born in Kansas and I plan to die in Kansas!

When I travel out of state, I am teased about my name, Dorothy from Kansas. The next question from people out of state, "You do have a dog named Toto?" My reply was, "I have had lots of dogs, but never one named Toto!"

I thank God for my extended family; I have been adopted by Carol's family years ago and have spent lots of time with them over the years. Carol and I have been life-long friends, and her family came as a "packaged deal!"

Most of Carol's family lived in Kansas City, so when I took nurse's training there, they spoiled me when I was homesick for the farm and my own family. I really appreciated the attention, and to this day they still spoil me as they know I am away from most of my family due to deaths. All of Carol's brothers and sisters are still living. I have been invited to their family camping trips and vacations. They provided much of my sunshine over the years. We have lots of laughs as we visit and share pictures and other memories.

My brothers and sister had a good sense of humor, and they kept the laughter flowing. After I married Loren, with his ability to keep everyone on their toes, things only got better. Loren, with my brother's help, would tease everyone in sight. It is those memories that keep my sunshine brightly streaming!

Loren had a great family also; they took me into their lives with open arms. His sisters, Dorothy and Nellie, are still alive; Mable Jean passed away a few years back. Lives are always changing, and we have to learn to roll along and grab our rays of sunshine wherever possible.

The best time of my life was when Loren and I started raising our own family. We were unable to have our own children, but thanks be to God, we were able to adopt two fine babies.

Lorna Mae came to live with us when she was six days old. She was the sun in our life, and the next three years were spent searching for an American boy!

J.B. (James Bryan), a blue-eyed, red-blooded American boy, came to live with us when he was ten weeks old. Then our family was complete. We were so happy to have two kids, a farm, jobs in town (to get money to bring home the bacon), friends galore and the world by its tail.

Raising our kids, improving our farm and looking out for Loren's parents and my mother kept us busy. But back then, the busier I got, I happier I became. We always made time for everything; as the old saying goes, "If you want something done, find a busy person!" They will work it in to their busy schedule and complete the task.

My nursing career was accomplished around my family affairs, and sometimes my family got managed around my work. I worked in nursing homes, less than a full-time schedule, but the "on call" ruptured our family fun at times.

While my children were growing up, I worked as the Director of Nursing in a couple of nursing homes so as to have a flexible work schedule. You may have guessed, many of my work hours were done during the middle of the night when my kids were in bed and Loren was at home. But that was okay, as I was young and tough at the time. I couldn't take that rugged work detail today!

Most mothers burn the candle at both ends and let the wick run out in the middle! My wick would run out quite often, but I would stop, "regroup" and start all over again. It was the funny happenings in my life that helped re-supply my wick.

11

OVER THE YEARS many conversations started with, "Now you're a nurse!" In my mind, I would think, "Is that a question, a statement or a complaint?" But I would just acknowledge their remark with a simple reply, "Yes!" and a big smile.

To this day, I have not figured why so many people have said that to me, but I usually enjoy it each and every time. I often wonder if people in other professions find a similar remark as the standing ice breaker to get free information.

I live in a rural setting and there are very few registered nurses in the area and no doctor for many miles, so I have been the local information booth, Free of charge, of course! They seem to think that I remain open at all hours, as they call me for information and free house calls.

When I retired from full-time nursing, I changed my local profession services. I started charging for house calls, and the word soon got around that the local free information booth had been closed. When this book hits publication, the word will be out about my purpose. I do one home health patient daily, and if she dies before I do, I will be fully retired.

Years ago, one little old lady called me to use my enema bag!!!! So help me, God, that is true. I kindly explained to her that I did not furnish nursing supplies to the community and suggested that she have her daughter go to the drug store.

When I got off of the phone, I just fell out laughing, and

Loren wanted to know what was so funny. When I told him, he said, "Do you think they ask the local lawyer to use his brief case for the weekend when he isn't working?"

It must be the personal touch that nurses deliver that makes people at ease to ask for extra personal equipment to go with the free nursing advice.

My neighbor has a cute expression when I ask him, "How are you?" He replies, "If I were any better, I would have to take something for it!" I added, "You know about my 'healing hands' and you do not want me to touch you!"

Over the years at one time or another, people have asked me some astonishing questions. I am of the personality that I usually have an answer off of the top of my head, exercising my wit. However, I am careful as to whom I give crazy answers. Lots of times my crazy answers have been under my breath and shared later with Loren for an evening laugh.

Since I have become a widow, I talk to myself and to Loren, as he is always in my spirit. I laugh and imagine what he would say if he were here in body and mind. I share most of my laughs with Carol via tapes and wait impatiently for the return tapes. Sometimes the laughter gets lost in the mail.

Laughter is my advice for survival! I catch a sunbeam and spread it where I can to help another person to laugh and enjoy life.

One of my friends gave me a plaque that reads, "When you are at the end of your rope, tie a knot and hold on!"

It was the laughs in life that kept me holding on to the rope — I am going to share the random memories of the unusual experiences during my life.

****

My first and last experiences are very clear in my mind. When I graduated from nursing school, I hired on at a local federal hospital. The hospital is world-known for their psychiatric treatment because of their affiliation with Dr. Karl Menninger who was world-renowned.

My first day at work, insecure and scared as a bunny, I went to the hospital cafeteria alone for lunch. As I was ordering a sandwich, I turned around to go to the table; a patient doubled up his fist and swung it right past my nose, missing me by a hair. As he swung, he said, "There she is — God damn her!" Then, he walked away.

I went over to a table to sit down, as I really needed to do just that! One of the male nursing assistants came over and explained, "He won't hurt you, he just scares new nurses!" I thanked him as I mumbled, "That he does!"

Many years later, I encountered another psychiatric patient as I was leaving the hospital for the last time. I must have walked through a patient's hallucination, as he jumped up when I walked out of the front lobby and yelled in my face, "I'll not go anywhere with you, NURSE!" I slowly continued my journey out of the hospital, and under my breath I said, "I do not want you to go with me as I have quit and are leaving you all behind!" He sat back down, and I left for good.

For the first few years of my career I worked on a geriatric, psychiatric unit. Many times my throat would tighten and my mind would question if I would survive the encounter. But as you see, I did and live to write about mainly the good times. Many times things are as funny as they were scary at other times. For the last twelve years as a federal nurse, I worked on an acute medical ward. Many of the patients were psychiatric with medical problems. I had my share of mental patients which are a real challenge.

I have been bitten, kicked, slapped, spit on, threatened and had my teeth knocked out of my mouth. Thank God they were false and not broken. I had a fat lip and a bad bruise. I was never hurt bad, just wounded my pride at times. I always prayed that next time I would be in a better position and not get hit.

One night I took a knife away from a little drunk who threatened to cut me. Then I had to call the guards to come and get the knife and dispose of the contraband properly according to federal regulations and document the affair. The guard asked me, "What happened?" I replied, "I told him to stay in bed as he was unsteady on his feet to prevent falling. He pulled the knife, and I took it away from him and put him back to bed." The guards were surprised that I was able to do so, and I exclaimed, "He is a lot littler than I am and I did not want to be cut!"

We had some wild episodes at times and most of the time a good staff to diffuse the situation. Many times we held the patient down until more medicine was obtained or a different type of restraint was available.

My first ward experience on my first day in 1957 as a graduate nurse was out of sight! You have to picture one long ward with twenty-five bed patients and no privacy curtains. All of the patients were mentally and physically incapacitated males; most were bed-to-chair patients. The nursing assistants in the essence of keeping patients clean would go down the ward and pull the sheets to the bottom of the bed, clean up the patient and move on to the next bed.

I was taught to use drapes and provide privacy. Can you imagine how shocked this country gal was on her first day on her first paying job in the city? To make matters worse, one of the patients cried all day, "What am I doing here?" Believe me, that was my question at the end of the day.

By the second day, someone had told the crying patient my name; then he yelled, "Help me, Miss Eastman. What am I doing here? Help!" In learning a new job and new responsibility, I really had to concentrate on what I was doing instead of what I was hearing.

On that ward there were several male nursing assistants, and their fun comprised of teasing the nurses, especially the new ones like me. I guess it was the "perks" of the job!

I was great material, as I was not only new, but I had no experience with "Ole Vets" and their surroundings. I caught on fast as it was survival.

We had a patient named Jack who wanted a cigarette more often than allowed. When he couldn't have a cigarette, he would ask the nurses for "a piece of pussy!" Most of the nurses would give him piece of candy which pleased him. He got so fat, we had to limit the candy. One day he, Miss Running Bear (a nickname for the black nurse — can you believe who named her that and why?) and I were walking down the hall, and he started his routine requests. We had no tobacco or candy with us, so he asked for "a piece of pussy!" The large black maiden nurse wore a rubber Playtex girdle and had a habit of pulling the long leg of the girdle out away from her body and letting it go, making a sucking sound against her fat leg. As she let the girdle go, she giggled! Jack said to her, "What the Hell is the matter with you — are you crazy?" You guessed it — the male aides named her that because of the nervous habit she had pulling on her girdle. They would say, "There goes Running Bear sucking air!"

The man I later married was a nursing assistant and one of the main tricksters, but a real treat to work with on a daily basis. Loren knew how to handle people and how to diffuse the problems while protecting all who was around him. He was truly a joy to know and to have on your nursing team. I imagine that is what made me want to have him around in my life.

When the patients were not "acting out," the nursing assistants were thinking how to "rattle" the nurses and get something going for fun and excitement. That way life on the ward was never dull for anyone, especially for the nurses.

Another patient comes to mind during the first few weeks on the job. This patient would repeat what he heard over and over. Some of the ornery assistants made sure that he heard a phrase that would keep the nurses on their toes. One of the assistants told him my full name, as they knew he would add his name behind mine and keep repeating it all day. He insisted on calling me all six names each time I was close to his bed. No way could I convince him we were not related; then I caught onto the trick.

After I got used to the nursing assistants and their pranks, they gave me a break and started including me in their fun and games from time to time.

I still associate with many of the good friends that I was fortunate to meet while working on the unit where I began my career as a registered nurse. In fact, many of the women are still alive and attend my monthly book reviews that I have in my home.

One scene comes to mind. As a young curious nurse, I tried to learn from my co-workers' expertise. I was trying to collect a urine specimen from a patient who would not cooperate. One of the experienced male aides said, "Let me talk to him in his terms!" They went to the bathroom, and I listened to learn his technique. The aide handed the urine bottle to the patient and said, "Go piss in this bottle!" The patient handed back the bottle and said, "Go shit in the creek!" No urine sample was collected that day, regardless of the technique. I learned that any one technique does not always work on any given day!

There were always lots of good "Ole Vets" that appreciated your care and your concern for them. They make the rough spots smooth out to some degree. One night a dying cancer patient called me a "rare fruit jar!" I laughed, as I thought he was teasing me about my weight. I had a good laugh and proceeded on my rounds. A few days later while reading his obituary, I found out that he was a glass collector and an expert on antique fruit jars. In fact, his research had been published in many periodicals and magazines. Then I knew his compliment to me was bigger that I had assumed at the time!

****

The following episodes do not connect to each other, but they connect to me. With these random accounts of the fun and laughter, I had a great life and career as a nurse. I enjoyed the new words of my children and my grandchildren, and I feel that I must enjoy them twice as much by accepting Loren's share. I have had more than my share of laughs, and I have tried to give my patients, family and friends a good laugh whenever time permitted and when my sense of humor was willing.

I have created many smiles on the faces of my ill patients; I tried never to use my humor inappropriately. I tried to "go easy" on the surgical patients to prevent them from ripping our their stitches! As a corny nursing student, I was caring for a post-operative gall bladder patient. I was trying to get her to move about in bed to relieve herself of the postoperative abdominal gas. She had noisy relief and I made a statement, "You could open up a gas station and make some money!" Needless to say, she enjoyed my idea and gave a big belly laugh. The thought crossed my mind, "I'll be in hot water if she rips a stitch and the surgeon and the nuns get a hold of me!" The Catholic nuns usually enjoyed my fun and games, but I was always cautious about my boundaries. You know this story is old, as surgery patients barely get to use the bed any more, let alone sit in bed long enough for gas to form.

****

One little dried-up veteran, who absolutely would not follow the physician's orders, kept coming to the hospital and doing as he pleased. One night his serum potassium level was at a critically low level, and he needed an intravenous feeding of potassium or death would occur. He just took the intravenous needle out of his arm and left the ward to smoke. The aide came and told me, "His IV was infusing medicine into the bed and he was gone." I sent her to the smoker to get him; it did not take a detective to figure out where he had gone — smoking was his first love! She brought him back to the ward screaming to the top of his lungs in the middle of the night. I once again explained the importance of the IV medicine to him. He replied, "No!"

The aide, who also was a robust farmer-type lady, and I lifted him out of the wheelchair and into bed. She held him as I restarted the intravenous medicine. We had to restrain him to save his life! During the procedure he threatened us bodily harm! Later we had a good laugh as we had been threatened before. When each nurse outweighs the patients considerably, you don't get too scared!

****

After we bought and moved our house to the farm, I wanted an attic fan put in, but Loren drew the line and said, "We can't afford any more at this time!" A few months later and lots of sweat, I called an electrician and a carpenter and had an attic fan installed one day when Loren was at work.

He came home and said, "I told you we couldn't afford any more things!" I replied, "It was cheaper than a divorce!"

"Besides, I am the one who will be having foot surgery, and I need some cooling!" He could not argue with that ,and later he had to admit that fan was the greatest invention!

****

Another "vet" who was dying of cancer had a wife with many mental problems, and his upcoming death would add to her unstable condition. One day I just finished giving him his bed bath when his wife came to visit. She later called back in a wild state of mind and accused me of touching his thigh. As I told the secretary who took her call, "Hell, I touched "everything" before she entered the room!" It is hard to give a bed bath without touching thigh, etc..... More than once she called back and threatened to sue me for showing affection to her husband, but when she was in the room while I was providing his care, she was sweet as pie!

Threats did not happened to me often, but they did arouse my sense of humor. I had to be real careful to wait for just the right spot on the ward to have my laugh. Many times my family would ask me why I was smiling or laughing when my mind was reliving the day's antics.

One threat was just as ridiculous when I was director of

nursing at a local nursing home. A prominent lady in that town put her mother in the facility after she had bragged around town that her mother would never go to the nursing home. She told me, "Do not take Mother out of her room; just leave her here for meals." I told her, "It is our policy to have everyone out of their room for meals and activities."

After word got around town that her mother was in the nursing home, she threatened to sue me. Of course, that was her way of dealing with the town's people when they mentioned to her about her mother being in the nursing home. Her lawyer never contacted me. I decided to laugh about the experience, but it never made me "hide" out any of my patients.

My philosophy: You have to live to learn about life! During my career, I was taught to listen to learn and learn to listen to do my job well. I guess I learned, as I survived a long career until my joints were squealing worse than the patient's family.

****

My mother rarely said anything funny. We kids got our sense of humor from our dad. Mother did have a funny saying when someone would ask about the make of car she was describing. She would say, "It must of been a Dodge as it was dodging right along!"

In the forties and fifties and as a kid, I could not understand why she didn't know the year and the make of the cars, as there were just a few styles on the market. I could not understand why she didn't know a Ford from a Chevrolet. But now with so many styles and makes of cars, I do not know all the styles by sight. I guess that is why the saying, "What goes around comes around!" is used.

My mother said another clever phrase when Dad would be in the barn, "getting his mules' attention." She said, "Your father will never die of a heart attack because he doesn't have a heart!" Mother never drove mules, but those who do say, "First, you must get their attention!" My dad was a real mule skinner in many people's opinion.

Dad was a farmer, but he turned "horse trader" every time he thought he could make a buck. Many times I heard Mother getting angry when Dad borrowed money to buy something that looked like a waste of time and money to her. One time, Dad bought some hogs that were so old they looked like long, skinny razor-back hogs. Believe it or not, the hogs got fat and Dad made some money.

Another time, Dad came home leading a real skinny horse that could hardly walk at the time. After months of my dad's tender loving care, the horse, Brownie, became our favorite riding horse and we rode him for years.

Mother failed to see the humor that we kids enjoyed most of the time, but later when we grew up and would tell stories around the kitchen table, I would catch Mother laughing to herself. So I said, "Mother, why don't you laugh at the time of the joke and let us kids know you enjoyed it, too?" She just smiled. But she never gave us the satisfaction of laughing at the time of the joke. I kept encouraging her to laugh with us and make our day.

****

When Bob, my brother, and I were real young, Mother would go after the cows. She would tell us to stay outside in case the house would catch on fire. In those days, we had wood-burning cook stoves and such. You know we were young, or we would have been going after the cows to be milked. Bob would tell me wild scary stories about Indians and Gypsies, we would get scared and go in the house to hide. Our favorite place to hide was under Mother's dresser, rolled up in blanket.

Needless to say, she was not happy with us upon her return. She did, however, know that Bob was good at telling Indian stories that he had heard from the older kids and community people, that he even scared himself.

Another scary thing with small children in those days were the stories about Gypsies stealing things, including small children. It is a wonder that any of us survived our childhood activities, especially the stories that were told. When we weren't being told wild stories, we were playing wild with the horses and other animals. We knew how to make our own fun even if it was dangerous.

****

Now I have grandchildren who light up my life and add to the humor. A few years ago when Jenny was five, I was on a low fat diet and remained on it for some time. Jenny questioned everything I did, and after she observed me staying on the plan and refusing the afternoon snacks that she was eating, she looked up at me and said, "Grandma, you are serious about this!"

I decided to teach her about proper nutritious foods. When she asked me to peel her apple and I said, "No, you need to eat the peeling for the fiber!" she ate the apple without further discussion. The next afternoon her four-year-old sister, Ashley, was here when we had an afternoon snack. Ashley asked for her apple to be peeled. Jenny quickly told her, "No, you need the fiber!"

Lorna, their mother, was here and she smiled at me as I sat there eating a banana. Lorna said, "Jenny, why does Grandma eat a banana every day?" Jenny replied, " 'Cause she likes them!" Again, Lorna smiled at me and said, "Oh, you haven't taught her about potassium yet?"

Being the daughter of a registered nurse, Lorna had heard the potassium replacement lecture many times when people came to our home to have their blood pressure checked. I would discuss the importance of eating bananas for a dietary replacement of potassium that their body had lost due to sweating or blood pressure control medication.

I still try to follow low fat and low sugar snacks, but it is hard for the grandkids to eat what is good for them instead of what they want. I must admit I have trouble with my own desires. WHAT IS GOOD TO US USUALLY IS NOT GOOD FOR US!

****

Jenny is 15 now, and the other day, she said, "Grandma, I made some applesauce, but it didn't taste like yours!" So I asked her how she made it and she said, "I put two packages of cinnamon red hots and some cinnamon in the apples." I explained that she put too many red hots and didn't need cinnamon with the red hots. Hopefully she will try again, as all of my grandchildren can eat their weight in applesauce, my recipe.

****

I took the four older grandchildren to the funeral of one of our friends. Criss was quite small at the time and he got a little naughty, so I made him sit down by my feet until he straightened up. When I let him back up in the seat with me, he said, "Oh, I miss her so — what was her name?"

****

Austin at the tender age of 18 months crawled up his high chair and over the tray and was sitting ready to eat while I stuttered and watched him. I expected the chair to fall over at any moment and hurt him. Jean noticed I was scared and she said, "Austin, are you trying to give your grandma a heart attack?" Then she turned to me, "Oh, he does it all of the time!" He was in place and ready for his ear of corn. He watched his mother buttering the corn, so he got ready to eat! He chewed that corn off of the cob and squealed for more.

****

When Taylor was smaller, I gave him an all-purpose pocket knife with a screw driver and small crude saw blade to play with while we were outside. The older kids and I found the tool/ knife when we were at the lake and it had laid in my trunk for a long time. I cautioned Taylor to make sure we got the tool put up so it wouldn't go through my mower. He put it up all right, and after he had left I thought of the tool and wondered where he put it? I never found it but mowed a couple of times and never hit it, which I felt

66

was pure luck. Finally I found it on a ledge in the garage in plain sight.

I let him play with it the next time he was here and gave him the same instructions — put it up so I won't mow over it. He did, and days later I found it in the china hut. Putting it up with my best china must have been his idea of safety.

****

Kids say and do the darndest things!

Morgan loves to take a tub bath when she stays with me, as they have only a shower and she likes to play. When I made her finally get out of the tub, she said, "Momma says, 'Wash your butt!' " I said, "And did you?" She said, "No!"

I love kids as they are so honest!

****

Jean took Morgan to the local library, and the librarian told me later that Morgan just sat down and was more or less talking to herself as she said, "This is where my Grandma checks out her books!"

When Morgan stays with me, she is always looking at my flowers and the beauty around her, which I feel is most unusual for a child of five. Many times she has remarked, "The country is so beautiful, I wish we could live out here!"

****

When Lisa was small, maybe five or six, we planted a peach seed to see if we could get a tree growing. I put a wire cage around it and kept it watered. One day I put the potatoes and carrot peelings and other garbage water on the tree for fertilizer. Lisa was with me the next time I watered it, and I asked her if she remembered what kind of tree we planted? She thought and looked at it and the peelings were still evident. She looked at me and said with a question in her mind, "A vegetable tree?"

****

When J.B. and Lorna were small, they slept in the basement, and we showed them how to take out their windows in case of fire. One evening when it was mighty cold outside, we had company. All of the kids were in basement, and they all filed in the front door. I looked at Loren and he looked at me puzzled. In unison we asked, "What are you kids doing?" J.B. said, "We are having a fire drill!"

Loren said, "If you broke that window, you'll think FIRE DRILL!"

****

Years ago, Loren and Tony Young would have me on the outside of the pig barn as they castrated the little pigs. When they were done, they handed me out the pigs to put down with the sows. I had to hold the door to keep the sows from going into the barn after the guys who were making their pigs squeal. To say nothing of protecting myself from sows!

One day I could not help them, so they had to fix up a better barricade between the sows and the cutting job. They hung their sweatshirts out in the corral up on a high post. The sows got the shirts down and tore them to bits and pieces. After the job, they looked for their sweatshirts and could only find pieces. Loren allowed they had me in a rough place, so after that I got to stand inside the barn and hold the door to keep the sows out and watch my arm as I lifted the pigs over after their surgical procedure.

****

My family did and said some funny things at least I thought they were funny. My oldest sister, Bessie, was a scream most of the time, and I will try to do a tribute to her to the best of my ability. In fact, when it came time to bury her, I did her eulogy because I didn't think anyone around here knew her as I did. She had just moved to Harveyville a few years before her death so I could watch over her.

My daughter-in-law, Jeannie, asked me, "How could you get up in front of a crowd and talk so well?" I told her, "I knew Bessie better than anyone around Harveyville, and she had lived away from Eskridge since she was 18 so few people knew the real Bessie! Besides I can talk easy; getting me to shut up is a real problem!"

Bessie had a heart as big as all out of doors! She would give a person the shirt right off of her back and she did many times, even if it caused her hardships. She was very gullible, and did door-to-door salesman ever capitalize on that trait. It appeared she believed everything a stranger would tell her, and salesmen told her plenty.

I lived with her after I finished nursing education, and that was the first time I had lived with her as Bessie went out to work before I was big enough to remember. She was 17 years older. I did stay for the summers to work at Purple Cow. Living with her full-time and sharing expenses, I soon found she could spend my money as fast as she could hers.

I was working the afternoon shift at the hospital, and a vitamin salesman had called on Bessie to sell her some vitamins. She really bought his sales pitch and had him wait until I returned from work to sell me his wonder vitamins, but I wasn't that gullible.

Since I was fat, Bessie assumed I would be interested in his "miracle fat cure." He attested that taking the vitamins would decrease my appetite so I would eat less. I knew for a fact it would take sudden death to decrease my appetite for good.

I asked the cost of the vitamins and he said, "Only $20 for a month's supply!" Let me remind you, it was the year 1958, and I could buy all the vitamins I could swallow in a month for $2!" I remarked to him, "Yes, I would lose weight as I would be spending my grocery money on vitamins!"

The salesman left and Bessie said to me, "Just stay fat then!" and I did. Guess what? She stayed fat also and took the expensive vitamins!

Bessie was wearing health shoes, a God-awful black shoe with a cuban heel. They did nothing for her health or her appearance! When wearing the shoes, she would occasionally turn her ankle. I kept telling her, "Those health shoes are going to cause you to break your neck someday!"

One evening we were walking down the street eating candy and laughing. Bessie turned her ankle and limped over to the plate-grass window at the Kresge Five and Dime store and hit her head on the window. I said, "Those health shoes are going to kill you!" A little old lady passerby said, "Oh, honey, did you get hurt?" I replied, "Naw, she just hit her head!"

Bessie and I had a good chuckle at the incident, and she said, "You damn fool, she will think that we have been drinking, and we are just eating candy and having a good time!"

Laughing at Bessie's shoes has come back to haunt me more than once as I aged and needed sensible shoes for my tired aching feet. Once I bought a pair of cheap back shoes for around the farm. J.B. wasn't very big, but he spotted those shoes from a distance and yelled, "Where did you get those u-u-u-u-u-ugly shoes?" That was not the only time I ate a plate of crow!

Just a few years ago I had a heel spur, so I bought some shoes that were good for my feet and hard to look at! After I bought them, I put them on and went to Hypermart to shop but decided to sit down for a cup of coffee. I did a survey; nearly every old lady coming in the store was wearing ugly shoes just like mine. Every other lady was also using a cane, walker or wheelchair. I taped Carol and told her it was a matter of time before I got my walking aide, whatever it might be. But my feet got better, I went back to fairly pretty shoes and haven't needed the cane yet, thank God!

I took Bessie to a nice restaurant in Kansas City for a good chicken dinner. She went to the restroom, and when she returned to the table she told me she used the wrong "john" and some little boys had to help her. I chuckled and said, "What happened?" She said, "Those rooms were marked "chicks" and "roosters." I guess I got confused since it had been so long since I was a chick!" I reminded her, "You have never been a rooster!" She said, "I was today!"

Years ago we had relatives who believed in a different religion than we did. When I drove Bessie to their farm, she noticed a lantern hanging up in a tree in the yard. After we left, she remarked, "They sure do get their light from above!" I asked her what she was talking about ,and she said, "Didn't you see the lantern in the tree?" She could make fun out of anything but, thank God, she waited until we left to make the jokes. Brother Bob always made the jokes in the presence of those he was joking about but not in their hearing distance, just mine, so I would giggle and brought attention to me instead of him and his wise cracks.

I am going to tell you one more thing about Bessie and then let her rest in peace. She loved gadgets — price was no object! She would buy everything, not only for herself but for anyone she thought would need the item. One time she bought J.B. a $20 fishing lure (this is when J.B. was a teenager) that was supposed to play a tune when he caught a fish! He said he never heard the $20 tune and he caught lots of fish, so he did not feel he got Bessie's money returned in music.

Just a year before Bessie's death, a salesman came to her door and sold her $300 worth of meat ,or at least that is what she paid for it. He just came to her door and told her he had a real "bargain," and she bought it for our Christmas. He told her someone else had ordered it and didn't have the money; she wrote him out a check … My kids and I had some mighty good steaks because of the goodness of her heart. I have no idea what the steak cost a pound and neither did she. Maybe she knew it was her last Christmas and she rewarded us for helping during her declining years.

****

I have been teased many times over the years about my fast walking pace with such short legs. There is reason for my fast pace, and it was stimulated by my father, years ago. He believed in getting the job done! One time when I was helping Dad in the corral, he tapped me on the back of the legs for walking too slow. Now you figure that out — I was ahead of him! One thing for sure, I have been a steady walker ever since. Loren used to ask me when we were going to walk somewhere if we were going to walk or go on that "ole nurse's trot"? I informed him that I learned that little quick hop down on the farm, but it did come in handy in my career. But age and time has slowed my pace, I never hurry anymore — it doesn't pay!

****

When I was director of nursing at a local nursing home, I admitted an older gent, but he had the "youngest" eyes I have ever seen. Now picture this scene, I was a middle-aged chubby nurse, but the way his eyes undressed me as he scanned my body from head to toe made me feel naked! I took him to the local physician's office for an examination and orders so we could give him proper care. The doctor had not seen him for years, so I was telling about his current physical abilities. I told Dr. Paul, "He is hard of hearing, but he has the youngest eyes I have seen. His eyes may be 92, but they look you over as if he was 18!" Dr. Paul rolled his eyes as he stated, "God, I hope that happens to me!" I responded, "The way you act now, I have no doubt!'

Funny remarks and happenings of the day kept me flying high for years. Without my sense of humor and the enjoyment of others' humor, nursing and the heavy demands of the profession would have been too difficult for me.

****

When Lorna was young, we got her a three-speed bicycle with a narrow banana seat. We were up the road at the neighbor's house and I decided to ride her bicycle home and let her ride home in the truck with her dad and J.B. It was about a mile home and downhill part of the way, so I thought that little stretch would be just right to renew my bicycle skills and try out the new bike. Wrong ... the distance was too far, the seat was too narrow, my butt was too wide and my body was too heavy. By the time I got home, the seat had cut me clear to my navel, so it seemed. I never rode another bike with a skinny seat! Boy, I like comfort and realized that I must leave the kids' toys to the kids. You can bet my bike has an old-fashioned seat — solid comfort.

J.B. bought his motorcycle when he was sixteen; I knew my legs were too short to reach the ground when I wanted to stop, so it killed my desire for riding his cycle. I also knew he was not large enough to hold both of us up if I tried to ride with him. I guess I finally grew up!

****

I thought I had grown up, but I must have missed a lesson here and there! After I was fifty-five, I tried a ride at the Kansas State Fair in Hutchison. I read in the local morning paper about this ride where you could see all the fair excitements from the air. That sounded good to me as I wanted to look the place over. The paper failed to mention that you would need two people to a seat if you wanted to see anything but "stars." My older friend, Bob Snickles, got in one seat and I got into another so as not to look like young lovers and be smashed in one seat! The ride looked calm as we watched before riding, but remember, there were two people in each seat when we were watching. The ride went up into the air and then shifted to the side, went down, shifted over to the other side. This pattern continued for several times before stopping.

Can you imagine what happens to one body alone in a seat? I started with a firm grip on my purse in the seat beside me. When the ride caused me to slip over, it crushed my purse with a mighty wallop! I thought about my purse containing my glasses and I would be unable to work the next day without my glasses, so I had to move my purse one way or another before the next big quick slide over! With these worries and sliding from side to side, I did not see the other attractions that I went up in the air to see.

Needless to say, the kids behind me and the operator were enjoying watching Bob's and my butt on the move each round. See if I ever read the newspaper again as to what ride to take! I am an avid newspaper reader and always read to check on the events when I have time to try new and different things. I vowed to do more research when trying new thrills.

After the above experience, I thought of what a patient had told me shortly before. I saw this little old man come out of his hospital room early in the morning holding his back. I said, "Is your back hurting?" He smiled at me and said, "Honey, I just have a few parts past warranty!" I gave up fair rides so as not to hasten the warranty on my parts.

*******.***

Years ago when my grandmother, Annie Eastman, was alive, I would shuttle her to and from Aunt Ruth's house to my mother's house, as none of them drove a car. While crossing town with Grandma, we saw a man watering his lawn with a garden hose. Grandma said, "He sure has a healthy stream!" I was shocked, I have heard lots of male patients and doctors talk about "their stream," but not my Grandma!

****

Bob and I grew up in spite of our fun and games; we survived our childhood capers and lived to tell about it. But we were cautious as to what we shared with our kids when they were young, and I watched our young kids like hawks as I had a good memory. We made our own fun, no matter how dangerous it was at times.

With our parents gone for the day, Bob asked me to find the shells for the old double-barrel shotgun. So I did! He said he would try it first and then I could take my turn! Did I mention? This gun was minus most of the stock? Bob shot the gun — the gun flew up in the air, and Bob landed on his butt! Needless to say, I did not take my turn.

****

My life continued to have strange and funny times, for which I am grateful. A few years ago while leaving a theater in Branson, Missouri, a total stranger looked at me and asked, "Did you go to the bathroom?" I must have glared at him thinking, this is a first for me! He continued to say, "Well, go to the bathroom — it is world-renowned!" The stranger made sure that my friend, Bob Snickles, knew that the male restroom was also the world's greatest bathroom. Both of us turned around and checked out the restrooms. My, the women's area was a sight to behold. Gold-plated faucets, large individual stool areas, each big enough for fancy dressing rooms. Floral arrangements and decor that made the area far too loud and pretty to allow rest. I started out my life using an outside shanty and never dreamed of ever seeing such elegant accommodations.

****

As the night charge nurse on a medical hospital floor, I went to the bathroom and told the aide (an English war bride) that I was going to the library for a few minutes. My supervisor made rounds while I was in the bathroom, and the aide told her I went to the library. Later the supervisor questioned, "Why did you leave the ward?" I had to think for minute, then the slang for bathroom came to my mind. We all had a good belly laugh after I explained to the supervisor and the English aide that I was speaking of the bathroom, as I planned to read for a minute or two. The laugh helped us make it through the night.

For those of you who have worked the graveyard shift, you know how hard it is to make it through some nights, as staying up at night is against Mother Nature. I have had to explain my slang and actions to more than one supervisor during my career. Sometimes they laughed, and sometimes they lacked my type of humor, but that was their problem. I usually got out of hot water with my explanation.

****

As you read, you more than likely have guessed by now, I grew up in a funny family, but I had just begun to know fun when I married Loren. He was everything to me. He made me laugh, and we shared our good life with others.

Our farm turned out to be a real funny farm.

We had a regular indoor bathtub in the pig pen as a water tank. That alone was funny to us, as both of us were grown by the time we had indoor plumbing and now our pigs had modern conveniences or at least a bathtub. The tub just sat there causing smiles, and when the pig crawled in, that really "turned on" the neighbors and relatives. Some friends were sitting in the shade by the barn, and they discussed the tub and pig activity when one of the barn cats came out and mounted the little dog! David said, "This is the funniest farm that I have visited in a long time!" Loren replied, "We don't even charge admission; stick around as it could get wilder as the day goes on!"

****

Now I have seven grandchildren that make me smile, and they help me to form new memories every day that I spend with them. I enjoy them as I did their parents, Lorna and J.B., many years ago. In fact, I try to enjoy them on Loren's behalf, and I tell them about their Grandpa Loren. As Morgan will say, "Was he my papa?" When I talk about Bob Snickles, she also asks, "Was he my papa?" I tell her, "No, Bob was just a good friend to Grandma and we went places together after Loren died!" Small children are so honest; they say just what is on their mind.

When Lisa was in kindergarten, she was staying with me until time for her to go to school. She was sitting eating her lunch, and she looked at me and her eyes got big as she told me about the accident of one of her classmates. She said, "His arm bone came right out of his elbow — they had to put veins in it!" I said back to her with big eyes, "That's too bad!" Her eyes got bigger and she said, "Yes, it is!" I had to stifle my laughter until after I took her to school.

****

In our school district we had a child in special education who required a paraprofessional daily. His name was Matthew. I was asked to work at the school one day as a registered nurse to do part-time nursing. It was the first day I worked in the district and I was his paraprofessional, which was a new experience for me.

Seeing me with Matthew must have impressed Lisa. After school, Lorna asked me to bring Lisa and Ashley home after school and she would pick them up later. Lisa was trying to express herself, and I was having trouble figuring out what she was saying. Then it dawned on me that she was saying, "You were Matthew's paraprofessional!"

I really enjoyed that, as I knew she had no idea what a paraprofessional was and she could hardly say the term well enough for me to guess what she was saying.

I guess it is a sign of the times! I had only heard the term for a short while, and I had to figure out what it meant as it is not in my Webster Dictionary or my Taber Medical Dictionary.

It has been fun to watch the change of times, and have I seen many changes over the last fifty years. Speaking of terms, the educators have put some words together for all of us to learn to pronounce and figure out their meaning.

Many people like little Lisa just try to pronounce the words and never try to figure out their meaning, which makes life for the rest of us very interesting and give me many chuckles.

****

When Ashley was eight years old, she helped Bessie and me stir up the community. Many people learned and we all had some good laughs. Although the laugh was on me, it never cost me any money. I paid lots of good money for entertainment that had fewer laughs!

When I finished Bessie's estate, there were several checkbook pads left. I hated to destroy them out right when the kids could do lots of writing and playing banker with them. Back then, Ashley, Jenny and Lisa could do lots of scribbling and tearing up paper in small pieces. The rule was for them to play and I would pick up the pieces and sort out the trash and destroy. I also gave them my junk mail to play school and have a good writing exercise.

My friend, Bob, was visiting, and he proceeded to scold me for letting them have them, and I assured him the kids would play and I would destroy them. He showed them how to write "Void" across the checks! We thought all bases were covered! I laughed at Bob as he worked with them to write "Void!" I said, "This is down home country, it is not the city — no one is going to cash them! Everyone knows Bessie is dead and her account is closed by now. These personalized checks are history." Later, I picked up the remains and burned them in the trash barrel.

One year later the kids in Ashley's class were learning to write checks at school. Ashley was a pack rat and, somewhat sneaky, she had put a checkbook in her purse. She took the checkbook to school and proceeded to write out a check for all of her classmates.

She learned the proper procedure (well kinda) of writing a check, but she forgot my lecture of the checks just being "pretend," and she ignored Bob's lecture about writing "Void" across the check.

You have guessed the rest of the story; one of the kids from the big city was unaware and took the check, $4.32, to the store and cashed it for candy.

My banker, Rick, said, "Have you heard about the check?" He laughed and said, "If I tell you, you have to laugh!" I replied, "If it is funny, I will laugh!" I sure enough laughed and said, "I can see Bessie laughing in Heaven and saying, 'I have been dead for over a year and I can still stir up that town with Ashley's help.' "

Then, I sat out to correct my mistake. I went to the store, and Mel showed me the check. It was written in pencil and signed by just Ashley with no last name, and it was personalized with Bessie's full name. I asked, "Who took this check?" Mel said, "It doesn't matter, we don't pay any attention when kids bring in checks!" I snickered, "Bet you will next time."

The parents of the kid who cashed the check paid for the candy.

Next, I called the school to alert the teacher, and she told me the principal alerted her and she talked to the class. I laughed as I said, "Did you remind them they have to have money in the bank before they write a check?"

Then, I called Ashley's mother and talked to Ashley, and she kept repeating, "I know — I know!"

One small town and an eight-year-old can further lots of people's education with one small check. Thank God, all of the kids didn't cash their checks and, thank God, the amount was small if I had to cough up the money. I have paid for other laughs with money and humility.

****

When Criss, my oldest grandson, was in pre-school, I was sure he was learning from his three older sisters. He brought pleasure to me from his eyes as they showed his innocence, but I was sure he would not be innocent long. Sure enough, at ten years old as he is now he can hold his own!

Criss is a typical boy — he never noticed my boot jack on the back porch until right after Christmas, and he had new boots when he was just a little tad. He watched me pull off my farm boots and said, "Let me try that!" His four-year-old legs were not long enough to hold the jack with one boot while pulling off the other boot, so I lent him help with a slightly longer leg. Keep in mind, my legs aren't very long, so I imagine we looked cute from the rear!

One day when I was using the ice pick, Criss became fascinated while watching me. I put the cover back on the ice pick and started to put it away. He said, "Let me see that!" I let him see it and put the cover back on and put it away as I said, "No, it is too dangerous!" He watched closely to see in which drawer it went. He never missed a trick back then, his big brown eyes rolling all of the time. His eyes say much more than his mouth does!

****

When Lorna and J.B were small, I worked part-time in a nursing home in Topeka. This allowed me to have flexible working hours and be more available for meeting our children's needs. I worked there for several years and the needs of my children became greater, so I quit my job.

All of the hospitals were thirty miles or more from our home, and they did not accommodate me with a flexible schedule. I was home only a few days deciding what to do and still be available to meet the needs of our growing children. I had not decided yet as what to do, and I got a call from a nursing home owner and administrator close to our home, only a few miles away. He was desperate for a registered nurse, but he was a small man with a big, bad reputation in our community.

His track record with women was not good; he had been highly criticized, but most nursing homes were under fire from all angles at that era in time. My personality trait is to observe and judge for myself as to the character of another human being, not paying much attention to local gossip. I didn't know him, just his reputation!

I accepted the job, and the nursing home had the capacity for fifty residents. It was far from being full to capacity, but I had to find out whether that was from poor management or the results of the community.

Let me tell you, I was being watched by the community then! One of the ladies in that town called the State of Kansas to see if I had a license, and she was told, "Yes, and in good standing!" That never ceased her from watching me like a hawk, and she tried her best to be my direct boss, but she didn't know my personality. I take orders from the guy that signs my check as long as his requests are on the up and up and, if not, I deal directly with him …

Three days after I began employment, the State of Kansas Nursing Home Inspectors came for a routine visit. Shortly into the inspection, I could tell that I had been hired by a "little crook!" Things he said and did during the inspections were not true, according to my observation.

But I would not quit anybody on the third day! Besides, there were many good employees that needed some direction to give proper nursing care to well-deserved residents. Needless to say, I kept my nose clean! I have worked for dishonest people before; I just told them I will work for you, but I will not lie for you! If I do not have enough staff people to do the work as regulations demand, I will not tell the inspectors that the work was done. I will tell them exactly what was done, and the deficiency will reflect such!

A few days after the inspection, I had gone out of the back door of the nursing home to take a short walk and breathe a breath of fresh air. I walked around and came in the front door; I wore sneaky nurse's shoes so he did not hear me enter the door. His back was towards the door, and for some reason I jabbed him with my finger into his chest and said in a low voice, "What are you doing?" He jumped sky high and came down looking at me. I knew right then he thought someone had a gun in his ribs! That confirmed my mind, I was working for a crook.

The "little crook" was also a womanizer, and the small community did not like his personal behavior. He told me he was going to marry one of the women he had been chasing, and he said, "Now I will put an ad in the local paper to read — Stud Service Discontinued!" I discouraged that ad, but he did not listen to my advice!

The announcement of his new marriage and his "Stud" ad appeared in the same issue of the local paper. Since I had just started working for him, I took quite a bit of teasing myself. Of course, teasing does not bother me, so that did not last long.

My naive friend asked me, "Does your boss have horses?" She quickly added before I could answer the first question, "Does he have dogs?" My reply was, "No!" She exclaimed to her husband who was riding in the front seat of the car with Loren, "He doesn't have dogs or horses!" We all laughed, and I guess she finally figured it out!

One day the town ceased to find anything funny about that little crook, as he left town with the State of Kansas welfare check and we never saw him again. There was no money as he had cleaned out the bank account, so all of the payroll checks bounced, as well as the checks that were paid to suppliers. The residents and employees were left behind to do without supplies or paychecks for doing hard labor.

The next few weeks were very difficult, but everything was eventually worked out with an ex-wife, and the business was sold. Life is just full of interesting experiences. One never knows what they will endure before completing an endeavor.

****

Working in a long-term care setting is much different than working in a hospital giving acute care. Spoon-feeding residents is much like feeding babies, but with a different size of the body. Nancy, one of the terrific aides, was feeding a resident, and the resident kept pushing the pureed food back out with her tongue. Nancy would patiently put the food back into her mouth. After several cycles with the same bite, Nancy exclaimed as she laid down the spoon, "I am done recycling that bite!"

Nancy was a very dependable person and usually had lots of patience, but there is something about pureed foods that can wear down your patience level!

****

I recall one of my first experiences with a geriatric/psychiatric patient. I was the charge nurse and a new graduate nurse with limited psychiatric knowledge. We were short of employees one evening, and we gave a shower to all of the patients, half of them one evening and the rest the next evening. I told the aides to put a cart of pj's in the day room and I would dress the patients for bed who were not having a shower; just good team work getting the work done with the staff available. After they got me a cart of pj's and I pulled down the shades, I started undressing the patients and putting on their pj's. It is my nature to move swiftly as I do my work; I move faster when short of staff.

One of the patients had a sock hanging out over his blue jeans, and I gave it a jerk to pull it out of his pants! He yelled, "You are jerking my peter off!" I was shocked beyond words in spite of him being a psychiatric patient! I examined him and sure enough he had a sock tied around his penis so tightly the end was blue. I never dreamed he had a sock tied attached to his body! An experienced nurse might have guessed why the sock was hanging there!

I ushered the patient into the shower room for the males aides to remove the sock and give him a warm shower. His brutal accusation was being repeated over and over again in my head, as I felt I had done him more damage than he had done himself. The aides took care of him and showed no excitement.

Later while I was charting the incident, I asked the males aides if he had any skin damage or if any trauma was apparent after his shower. I also asked them if they knew why he did this? They smiled and said, " He does it all of the time; we watch him closely!" I said, "Well, we must record and report this as he may have gangrene to the penis someday." They wanted to drop the issue, but I kept hammering away at them until I got the whole story! One of the aides finally told me, "He does it because it won't stand up any more so he ties it up!" Here, I thought he might be clamping it to keep himself dry! A naive country gal like me would have never thought of that! After duty and over the years, I have had many a good laughs over that experience. I love life!

****

Loren had an unusual way of expressing himself when he felt he could not afford an item. At least that is the way I saw it and remember him. When someone would suggest he buy an item, he remarked, "I couldn't buy a sweat jacket for a hummingbird!

That was just one of his unusual sayings that he repeated from time to time when the timing was just right for the occasion.

****

My theory on life's episodes never change, but the players change every few years! When Lorna and J.B. became teenagers and started thinking about sex and other things that all of us thought about when we were growing up, I tried to impress upon them, there is no new sex or tricks, just new tricksters. In other words, the same old tricks with new players.

My kids would look at me when I would approach them and express my concern about their recent tricks. I would explain to their questioning eyes (their eyes would say, "How do you know?") And I would look at them and express, "I was your age thirty years ago! I can still remember what was on my mind at that time!"

Loren was dead before J.B. truly knew the entire facts of life! He was not here to explain the male angle of life to J.B., so I did. I would tell him like I thought Loren would tell him. J.B. would look at me and his eyes would say, "YOU are saying this to ME?"

As a widow with children to finish raising and farm property to manage, I put on my jeans, pulled on my boots and took the place of "My Man" more often that I wanted to do so. I had to be strong and had to double as the male authority in our household whether I or anyone else liked it or not.

My sense of humor and the humor of Lorna and J.B. kept us going through the hard times. Many people asked me how we managed and I would reply, "Do we have an option?" It was not easy, but we survived and lived to laugh about the rough times.

****

There was a lot of difference in my college days compared to J.B.'s days in college. J.B. was unaware of my experiences while I was observing his and the great difference.

I had eye surgery while J.B. was home from college, so I asked him to drive me to the doctor's office for a re-check. After the examination I asked him to take me by the grocery store on the way home, as I wanted to buy fruits and vegetables for a basket for a ill friend. J.B. thought I was overdoing it with the amount of items I put in my grocery basket. He exclaimed, "If you were in college, you would learn to do without!"

I replied, "I was in college and I did do without!" J.B. rolled his eyes and said, "OH Jesssussss!" I added, "I did without a vehicle, I did without a T.V. — !" Then his eyes said, "Why did I say anything?"

I hope to be a little mouse and listen to J.B. and his daughter, Morgan, as they discuss Morgan's college disadvantages over his years ago! There will be many more changes in society and college in another fifteen years.

****

Jenny and I went to let her do her birthday shopping for her tenth birthday. We went to the same store where her mother and I took the children for school supplies earlier that year. During the school shopping, I took Jennifer outside of the store for a time-out and we sat on an outside bench until her attitude improved.

On the birthday trip, we were talking as we walked into the store. Jenny said, "I am your oldest grandchild and you always spoil me!" I said, "I do not!" Just as we passed the time-out bench, she said, "You always baby me!" I pointed toward the bench and said, "Remember the day that I babied you on that bench!" She smiled big and said no more.

****

I greatly enjoy dancing, and when I was younger I went dancing every chance I had. The nurses on the last ward I worked knew I was a dance enthusiast and would tease me about dancing with the guys on the ward. Most of the patients never took them serious. One day on nursing rounds, Nurse Shirley said to a bed patient, "Dorothy will dance

with you." He attempted to crawl out of bed, tubes and all."
Shirley quickly grabbed him and said, "Later!"

However, I did ask one patient to dance with me! While working on the night shift, I was determined to bring a ray of sunshine to one of the terminal cancer patients, so I said, "This is Saturday Night, do you want to dance with me?" His eyes beamed and his face lit up! It made me feel real good to provide him with that much pleasure on his death bed.

****

When working on the same veteran's hospital ward, I was admitting a drunken old soldier. I made the mistake of leaning over in front of him to get some pajamas out of the bedside stand. He grabbed both of my posterior cheeks in his hands and said, "You got a cute little ass!" I let him know such behavior was not acceptable and that I was not amused! I winked at the two sober guys who brought him to the hospital so they could at least enjoy part of their journey to the hospital with a drunken comrade.

****

While making a bed in a nursing home, a ninety-one-year-old resident was sitting close enough to tap me on the rear while I made her bed. I said, "You better watch that!" She replied, "Why, honey, will it go off?" That great line lit up my life and made my heavy load of nursing home care lighter that day. I have thought of it many times since.

Nursing home work is very hard, but some of the little old people in that setting have more spunk than one can ever imagine possible. Some of them keep the humor and laughs flowing for all to enjoy. Of course, the staff helps out all they can depending on their personalities.

My mind works overtime to create enjoyment and laughs for people around me, and that is a blessing in care homes. I have always been chubby, and that alone caused some smiles as my weight never inhibited me. As I was walking down the hall carrying an extension cord, I decided to jump rope for the residents to watch. I made several jumps before the cord got caught on the sprinkler nozzle in the ceiling. Thank God, I did not pull it out of place. I did tell the owner how I entertained the residents just in case the ceiling came down or the sprinkler sprung a leak! He knew me well, so he smiled and shook his head!

****

My most favorite workplace was a railroad hospital where I went to work two years after graduating and gained some psychiatric experience at the V.A. The railroad hospital took care of strictly railroad employees, not even their families. The hospital policy stayed as such until Medicare came into being and then people outside of railroad employees could not be banned from care. So many things changed at that time.

I worked for years in the outpatient clinic and emergency room, assisting eight doctors and taking care of emergencies and admissions to the hospital proper.

My first experience in that clinic came as I was the patient and getting my entrance examination. The head nurse, whom I will call Nurse C., was a classic. I learned first-hand how the patients must view the clinic, the doctor and the nurse! I wish the episode had been captured on video, but that was before videos were made!

I was waiting in the lobby for my physical. A man with a pipe hanging on his lip and his glasses way down on his nose walked out into the lobby and called my name. Here again, it was in the time before half-glasses. You may have guessed by now, I worked as a nurse before lots of inventions came on the market. Doctor Fred definitely needed half-glasses!

I followed Doctor Fred to the examining room, and he said the nurse would help me prepare for the exam. He left the room, and Nurse C. came into the room and rushed me out of my clothes and gave me a small towel to cover my chest. That was the days back when I was young and voluptuous! To myself I thought, "My God, that towel won't cover much!" But I did as I was told as I had been trained at home and in nurse's training to obey.

Nurse C. covered my bottom half with a draw sheet, Thank God! Doctor Fred came back into the room, asked me a couple of questions as he lightly touched my abdomen and listened to my heart. He muttered around his pipe as he looked over his glasses, "You need to lose some weight!" That was the end of the physical —. He left the room, and Nurse C. came back in and rushed me back into my clothes, girdle and all.

Again, I followed orders and did not mess up their routine, but my mind was saying, "Hell, he could have done that exam out in the middle of the lobby and I would not have had to hurry out and back into my girdle and bra!"

I asked the clerk, "Did I pass the physical?" She looked strange and said, "Well, yes ..." I knew right then I was in relaxed surroundings and I could have some laughs.

The next week I was working there, and I tried to create a different image to the patient than the one I had seen on my first time in the examining room.

One day, I was the only nurse working and I was very busy helping all of the doctors, Doctor S. said, "Put this patient in the rectal room," as he called the emergency room. We did all rectal exams in that room, as the lighting was just right for the job.

I told the young man, "Go into the emergency room and drop your pants and get up on the table on your left side!" He did, and I went in and draped him with a sheet and put the intensive light on his rear end, laid out the proper rectal equipment and left the room.

Keep in mind this was in the days when patients did just exactly as you asked them to do and never questioned your intent.

I went about my business with the other patients, as the doctors always did the rectal exams on the male patients unless they asked for your assistance. When I noticed the emergency room door open, I went in and Doctor S. was working on the young lad's finger.

Doctor S. started to "rib me" about making that young man drop his pants when he had a sore finger. I said to the young man, "Why didn't you tell me you were here because of a sore finger?" He smiled and said, "Because you told me to drop my drawers!"

I popped Doc with a towel and said, "Quit calling this the rectal room unless you are doing a rectal — I don't read minds!"

I immediately remembered my first clinic experience of how I was rushed out and into my clothes without any real need. It is good for the nurse to think and remember how the patients might feel and think …

That clinic had a variety of both origins and personalities so I really enjoyed working there and would have preferred to do my entire career in the clinic of that hospital. I have lots of fond memories and funny experiences from working there with the staff who were like an extended family.

I quit that hospital not once to adopt a child, but both times when we got Lorna and J.B. I never returned to the hospital work while my kids were young. Good family life and hospital schedules do not mix well.

When the kids were in high school, I left the nursing home setting and went back to work at the veteran's administration hospital where I started my career right after my training.

Twelve years later, I retired from floor duty and full-time work. Then I went to work with the school district in the city, and the work experiences were entirely different from all of my previous types of work.

I had lots of psychiatric hospital episodes but never any experiences with autism until I joined the school staff. The first time I had to medicate an autistic child, I gained new insight about autism. Good thing I had experience in psychiatric nursing, or I would not have been able to medicate that child. Many years later, I hope the people involved with their care understand their needs better than we did then!

School nursing gave me many new challenges. By personality, I rarely am speechless! Occasionally a patient will make my tongue idle. One of the small grade school students came to the clinic. He gave me his symptoms, and I said, "Lie down and I will check you over." He replied, "I can't lay down!" I asked more questions but never heard any answers that I understood. I again asked him to lie down and he refused. I stated, "You must be able to lie down at night so you can sleep." He said, "No —, I hang!"

That made me speechless as I did not know how to follow that answer! I was too "chicken" to ask if he hung like a monkey at night? He sat for awhile, and I looked him in the eye and suggested, "You are better now — maybe you want to go back to class!" He got up without another word, and I never saw him again. At the schools I came up with some "miracle cures."

****

One cute little girl came to the clinic with her nurse's pass; I saw her last name was Van Winkle and her teacher's name was Dalton. I do and say lots of things just to see the patient's reaction, as it quite often tells me more than their mouths say with their symptoms!

I asked the little girl if her dad's name was Rip? She just giggled, so I asked her if her teacher was one of the Dalton Gang? She giggled again, and by then I was sure she was not sick! So I waited a short time and sent her back to class.

The secretary asked "How did you cure her so fast?" I told the secretary what I had asked her and how I had watched for her reaction. The secretary stated, "That is a cool method — that child comes to the clinic a lot ,so I will have to think up new ideas for her!

****

I enjoyed the secretaries at most of the schools, as the clinics are usually next to the secretary's office. They are great help, as they know the children and I do not. The nods and eye movements of the secretary often help me to assess the student's needs easier.

****

During the fall season and the start of a new school year, the high school boys were wearing a new clothing craze! They wore their jeans or shorts, low — real low, the belt line was across the pubis. If you know your anatomy, there is nothing there to hold up your pants, so most of the boys held their pants up with one of their hands to keep the pants from falling to their knees! In providing nursing treatment for their complaints, some of my instructions required both hands to carry out the instructions. You guessed it — their pants fell to their knees!

As one of the black boys followed my nursing orders, his pants fell to his ankles and he had red undershorts beaming to the rest of the clinic. One of the black girls finished her treatment and walked behind him when his pants were down around his ankles. She smacked his butt and said, "Cover up your black ass!" He never even flinched! I never said a word as I was dumbfounded and speechless!

In that high school as most of them, the clinic is not next to the secretary's office. As I left work that day, I made a comment to the secretary, "I had a new experience today. Never before in my career did I have young men drop their pants without me asking them to do so!" I added, "I have had young men hesitate to drop their pants when I asked them, but not until today have I seen their bottoms without request!" The secretary only shook her head!

I was used to old drunks at the V.A, but young boys, supposedly normal, made me speechless.

****

A year or two before retirement, time had callused me to some extent! While working at the V.A., I became weary of old drunks coming into the hospital just to sober up and not for treatment of their real problem.

When I am weary, my choice of words is not always the best. In the middle of the night the admissions office called me to say they were sending me a patient with epididymitis, which is inflammation of the spermatic cord and testicles. The nursing staff must watch for swelling and apply ice as needed.

When I laid eyes on the patient, I could tell he came to "sleep it off!" But being the admitting nurse, I had to document whether or not he had swollen testicles upon admission.

I just said, "Drop your pants and let me see what you got!" Immediately, I knew I had used a very poor choice of words! The little drunk black patient put his arms up over his head so as to hide, giggled and said, " I'm not scared if you're not!" I quickly assessed that he did not need ice and left the room for him to sleep it off!

I shot out of the room so I could laugh and ran smack dab into the male aide that had brought him from admissions. You can bet he was laughing at my poor choice of words! Later the patient did not appear to have remembered my exact words, but the aide never let me forget them.

I do believe that being able to laugh at yourself while others are laughing is very therapeutic for the mind of everyone. Laughter is the best medicine, but there are times when it is inappropriate, and I have tried to refrain until the time and place are right.

****

Brother Bob had a drinking problem from early high school days and until his death. He would tell me, "I will drink and smoke until the day I die!" So he drank as long as he could make it to the liquor store, and he smoked as long as he could hold the cigarette. I would tell him, "Life is a choice!"

But Mother hated his drinking problem! After Bob was

an adult, he continued living at home with Mother until he got married. Mother's friends would tell her about his drinking episodes. She would say, "They said you were drunk Saturday night!" Bob would ask, "Who are they?" Mother would only repeat, "They said it!" Bob remarked, "If they would keep their mouth shut, you and I would get along better!"

Jack was the guy in our family that could really make you laugh with his ability to say things in a funny manner. Bob was right behind him, and together they were impossible. When they were with Clifford, business really picked up, and most of the time the three guys knew the score as to their jokes and the rest of us were the butt of their jokes! Bessie could hang in with them, and I imagine I could have as the years went by, but early deaths took many of them so I am left alone with my humor.

Jack was a real story teller, and it was hard to keep him on a serious subject for any length of time. He spent lots of his time "downtown with the boys," drinking beer and telling jokes, and he kept gathering jokes to share with the rest of us for a lifetime.

Besides the fun and laughter, another form of great satisfaction for me was the sewing of garments. I sewed for Loren, Lorna, J.B. and all of my family on both sides of the house. Most of the time they were very pleased with my success, as it improved their looks and the way they felt about themselves. Bessie lost a lot of weight when I lived with her, so I made her some sharp clothes. She put them on plus her jewelry and looked real spunky!

I made most of my clothes, as my size and shape were different than most of the ready-made clothes. When I was a young girl, what fit me was for a much older person, so I learned sewing out of necessity. I was very busy after marriage and raising a family, but would always have time to make a garment that I needed for myself or someone in the family. When they were pleased, I was very happy! The old saying goes, "If you want something done — ask a busy person and they will make time!"

Two cataracts later and great loss of finger dexterity, I do very little sewing. Besides, there are "fat shops" now and I can buy my clothes. After Loren's death, I found a "fat shop" in Manhattan called "Lots of Love," that would have done Loren in as he got such a kick out of my queen size hose, brand name, "Big Mama!"

Lorna still sews for herself and her children when time permits. I never taught J.B. to sew except for the basics such as buttons or such. He buys cute little tee shirts for Morgan and Austin.

I learned from my husband, who was in the Army, that men need to learn to sew the basics for button repair, etc. When I met Loren, I noticed that his shirt buttons were quite often sewn on with different-colored thread. After we got better acquainted, I asked why his mother did not use the proper color of thread when she sewed on his shirt buttons. He proudly said, "I sewed them on myself — besides, we only have black and white thread!" That impressed me that boys need to learn the basics for sure! I had never given any thought to a home without colored thread, but if no one sews, why have any colored thread?

****

We had a little niece, Lelia Jean, who had physical and mental birth defects. She needed lots of extras, so Loren and I would help her parents supply her special needs. I made clothing that would fit down over her braces, and Loren would make wooden equipment to suit her needs.

Lelia was very appreciative, and that paid the bill for us! She called me "Sugar" and, believe me, I liked that nickname. She was in a wheelchair and she called Loren "Ironsides," because of his size. We assumed she related to Raymond Burr who was a big actor in a wheelchair in the T.V. series called "Ironsides."

It takes a special person to think like that, and we were

proud to be in her family circle. She was a delight for all who knew her. She was funny and might say anything at any place or time. When she was alive, she kept the family on their toes just staying ahead of her. She was a very sick little girl, but such a inspiration for all who watched her survive her birth defects and complications for eighteen years.

****

I made Lorna anything she wanted, as she was small and I had scraps of material galore as I had been sewing for years before she came into my life. She loved to model the clothes I made for her as she "preened" around. It took so little to please her, just like Grandma Masters had said.

I also made clothes for J.B., but he did not like the "model phrase," so it was a real challenge getting his garments fitted. I made him some black tailored Western pants to match his father's slacks. J.B. refused to put them on so I could pin up the back seam to fit. He stated, "I'll not wear those pants with the butt out!" I had to talk fast to convince him that the back seam would be closed up when I was finished. He is a hard sale!

12

LIFE IS A REAL CHALLENGE, as I see life. If we look at it as a challenge instead of a chore, we have a better life. We must learn to laugh at ourselves. We must takes our jobs seriously but we need to take ourselves lightly! Laughter is important to survive life and it's many problems.

Everyone does not have the talent to relate funny stories but everyone has the ability to laugh at funny stories and it is good medicine for one's attitude. Everyone needs a good laugh quite often to succeed

"Humor is laughter made from pain, not pain inflicted by laughter."
— Author Unknown

Individuals with a good sense of humor and an ability to laugh at themselves seem to deal with life's adversities in the best possible way.

"A person without a good sense of humor is like a wagon without springs — jolted by every problem."
— Henry Ward Beecher

I try to remember that, "Success is a journey — not a destination!"
— Author Unknown

Therefore, I cannot quit trying to bring myself and others happiness as I continue to age and live the good life. Good health and happiness is the "Good Life" as I see life. Our attitude is what makes the difference. Good thoughts can do wonders for us at all times and fear of the unknown can keep us down.

"The fear of death keeps us from living not dying!"
— *Paul C. Roud*

I quit my good paying job as a full-time floor nurse in a local hospital after I realized that I lost my sense of humor. I am nothing to myself or others without my sense of humor.

After a good long rest, I went to work as a part-time school nurse. My supervisor heard my story as to my work record, and I was honest with her and told her I had lost my sense of humor with demanding floor care. She simply stated, "We will retread you!" And they did. Little by little my humor was restored. The following poem is food for thought. I found it posted in one of the first schools where I worked.

Outside my window, a new day I see,
And only I can determine the kind of day it will be.
It can be busy or sunny, laughing or gay,
Or boring and cold, unhappy and gray.
My state of mind is the determining key.
For I am the only person, I let myself be!
I can be thoughtful and do all I can to help,
Or be selfish and think just of myself.
I can enjoy what I do and make it seem fun,
Or gripe and complain, make it hard for everyone.
I can be patient with those who may not understand,
Or belittle and hurt them, as much as I can.

I have faith in myself and I believe what I say,
I personally intend to make the best of each day.

I am unable to give credit to the author of that poem, as it was a posted card but did not state the author. But the author helped me heal my wounded sense of humor. The much-needed rest before and only working part-time was also a big factor.

We all get busy when we get on the "merry-go-around" of success! We get so busy we forget to "stop and smell the roses" or to take adequate time for ourselves. It seems like everyone has to learn the hard way.

I did just that, so I quit work to rest up and reestablish my values in life. I had always professed that "Life is a Choice." I made my choice to give up a big salary and change my spending habits to concentrate on what is important to me. My happiness has always been important to me, and when I am not happy when I cannot laugh at myself!

Full-time nursing on a dead run with my aging process was taking its toll on my joints and mind. When one hurts all over, their sense of humor takes a beating.

I took the big plunge in life and quit work to start this book. Old memories surfaced when the body had time to rest and think good thoughts, such as the phrase I saw on restaurant place mats:

"Those who bring sunshine to the lives of others cannot keep it for themselves!"

I had always given sunshine to others, and I did not want to change in the later years of my career and personal life. I will relate how Loren, eleven years after his death, helped me to make to decision to quit full-time duty. Explained more detail in section, "Life is a Choice."

After working several years at the schools, I worked for a few months for a private home health agency until Loren's Aunt Minnie McMurdo needed care and I started taking care of her in her own home on a daily basis. Her vision diminished to the point where she needed daily help, so I help her which allows her to stay in her own home.

This book had taken me over seven years to write. First I just wrote down every memory I could think of, then started taking writing workshops and classes on how to write in story form again. After all, I documented facts in phrases on patients' charts for forty years, so sentence structure took some thinking and retraining myself.

13

I WAS A VERY LUCKY YOUNG WOMAN to have the experience of meeting a nice gentleman while working my first professional job. Not everyone is so lucky. As I have mentioned in other chapters, he and his work friends started teasing me on my first day at the new job as a graduate nurse.

Teasing was very much a part of my life before nursing. In elementary and high school in my home town of Eskridge, Kansas, I earned the description of being jolly, and I guess I lived up to their expectations.

Working in a hospital with mostly mental patients was a new experience for me. In training, I had three months affiliation at a psychiatric hospital, but being a graduate nurse is different. Besides getting acquainted with the new job and staff, I had to learn more about that type of patients than I had learned from my short tour at a psychiatric hospital as a student.

Loren and his friends were well aware that I was a "greenhorn," so they broke me in and quickly included me in their fun. I had to be careful, as the staff nurse is in charge on the nursing assistants and playing can lead the person in charge into "hot water" with the administration. We never got into any real trouble, but did we have fun after the patient care was given.

Loren asked me for a date, and I was in Heaven then! We dated for awhile, and I decided to quit that hospital and go to a local railroad hospital. It was a way to continue a relationship with the man of my dreams and be some other aides' boss! It was clear that men did not like their women to be in charge of them, on or off duty!

The scheme worked, as Loren and I were married one year later! I will never know whether or not he figured out my reason for changing hospitals! Maybe not, as I got to work in the emergency room at the railroad hospital, and that type of work was my kind of work I like best.

The reason I was so crazy about Loren was easy for other people to see, as he was a wonderful guy. He was the salt of the earth and a sincere fellow. His attitude and capabilities at work were outstanding. As a young nurse, I could easily see how he performed with the management of the patient's behavior. He was a smooth, solid man with honesty and great integrity.

Three years went by after we were married, and no children joined our family. I had one miscarriage, and my obstetrician doubted if I would ever give birth to a child. My nurse friend worked in the doctor's office. When Lorna was born and needed a home, she called me to see if Loren and I wanted to adopt a baby girl.

Then we were in "Seventh Heaven" and got the legal work done the next day. We had gone to the hospital to view that baby girl the night before, and she was beautiful to us.

Five days later when we got to bring her to our home, she was gorgeous! I will never forget the thrill. God did not allow me to bear my own children, but He did allow us good friends and the chance to adopt.

I can tell you that blood is known to be a tight bond between family members, but I know for sure that blood in not the essential element for a good bond! We bonded immediately to our adopted children, and there was no blood connection.

Loren and I had a happy life and a good marriage from the beginning, so when Lorna came to live with us we were ecstatic! We both were lucky to have good families, and they opened their arms and hearts to our adopted children. Lorna was the first adopted child in our families, as all of our siblings were fertile.

Holding and caring for a baby was most important to me. I had always loved babies and could not keep my hands off them. From the moment that Loren and I touched Lorna, she was ours! We acknowledged the word adoption because of its truth, but she was "our baby!"

A child made our marriage more complete. We loved each other but adored Lorna. I had my need to be a mother fulfilled, and Loren had two girls now. He acted like a man with his desires almost complete (he still needed a boy). He was as proud as a "peacock" when we walked down the street. A cute baby girl is usually the apple of their daddy's eyes. When she got big enough to roll her blue eyes at him, he would melt like butter.

I have always been grateful for our family unity. I believe in enjoying life as you go, as no one knows how long they will live! Loren and I played just as hard as we worked. We had lots of playmates!

When Lorna was three years old, we adopted James Bryan (J.B.), and then our family was complete. Now we had a precious little boy to join our darling little girl. Lorna enjoyed her new baby brother, and our life soared for years.

Lorna was six days old when we got her and she was a private adoption, so there was a period when her birth mother could have changed her mind and wanted the baby back. Then we would have been faced with a heartbreaking experience. Thank God that did not happen! J.B was adopted through the Kansas Children Service League Agency, so the final papers had been signed by his mother before he was released to us. He came to live with us when he was ten weeks old, after having lived in a foster home until the waiting period was over.

I am very grateful that we took the risk when adopting

Lorna and happy the agency helped us find J.B. A lifetime without children would have been sad to me as I love children. I am most grateful for my grandchildren who give me so much pleasure.

While raising a family, one gets pretty busy, but as I look back on my life, every bit of hard work reaped great rewards. When our kids were in school, their activities and our work schedules kept us coming and going. There were times that I had to stop and figure which direction I was going.

When J.B. grew past the baby stage, I asked Loren, "Can we get another baby? J.B. won't let me rock and cuddle him!" Loren said, "No, the insurance policies and everything is set for two kids!" Wasn't he just too darn practical! J.B. showed his sympathy by saying, "You'll have grandchildren!" Now, I have Austin to rock, as the rest of my grandchildren are too big to fit in the rocking chair with me.

Now that I have reached my present stage of life, I know for sure when my kids were growing up was the busiest time of my life and the most rewarding. The accomplishments were great and greatly appreciated.

Now Lorna and J.B. have children of their own, and now they know the joy of seeing their children grow. As the grandmother, I again enjoy watching the growing stages of my offsprings.

At this writing, Lorna is blessed with five children: Jennifer, Ashley, Lisa, Criss and Taylor. With the many details and projects of the children and her husband, Don Lawton, she definitely is in the busiest phase of her life. Now Lorna knows how she won Loren's and my heart from the moment that she came to live with us and became part of our family.

J.B. and his wife, Jean, had their first child, a baby girl named Morgan, and she is the apple of her daddy's eyes. Morgan put a new glow in J.B.'s gorgeous blue eyes that beams from ear to ear when in the same room. Like Loren, J.B. had two girls, and they are mighty happy. He is struggling to make a living, but I informed him that we all spent the first thirty years of married life trying to keep the bills paid. Four years to the day, Austin James was born, and now his family is complete.

Sports and activities were always important to our family. Many nights Loren and I spent as many hours on the bleachers as we did at our job on some days. Lorna helped with two high school teams, and J.B. played on the other two teams.

I have started my time on the bleachers again, only now as a grandmother, I can attend only the games I want to attend. I think going to and from school activities and discussing the events makes for some of the best family unity possible. After our children got big enough to drive to some of the events, I missed details and the family togetherness. Later, all of us were doing and thinking of other things, so details got lost in the shuffle. I am grateful that we had the time back then, and I live with the good memories now.

J.B. had real athletic ability. His father was blessed with a son who could play sports and play them well. Loren was an armchair quarterback, but his son was built for sports and played hard. Loren had the desire and the energy but did not have an athletic build. Loren was built to work and help others, just as I was built with a body like a work horse.

I told people that if God had wanted me to sit around and look good, He would have made me pretty!!! God also made me strong for other reasons, and I found them out when I lost Loren.

14

"IN EVERYONE'S LIFE, a little rain must fall!" so we can appreciate the sunshine and the good times. My life was going full tilt, but one phone call made me realize that my life may have taken a 180-degree turn. And it did! While at work, I received a call that Loren had been in an accident. His sister, Nellie, called for emergency suggestions they could do for Loren while waiting for the ambulance to take him to the hospital.

I met the ambulance at the hospital, and with one look I knew my world had turned around completely. Loren was dead on arrival at the hospital. When J.B. arrived in the next car, he told me that he and Uncle Bill had also been in the accident but were not hurt physically.

Lorna and Aunt Nellie arrived soon after J.B. It was an afternoon none of us will ever forget, but life goes on and we had to do just that!

The accident was caused by a car driving into the rear end of the tractor carrying a big bale of hay down the highway. J.B. and Bill were riding on the bale carrier as they were road-testing the tractor after Bill had worked on the engine. Since they were up the highway, Loren stopped and picked up a bale of hay from the field to feed the cattle. The tractor tire came off the medal hub from the impact of being struck by the car. The tractor rolled over, causing the metal hub to crush Loren's chest. J.B. and Bill were thrown clear of the tractor and other vehicle.

At the time the details of the accident did not seem important. I could see Loren was dead, but J.B. was alive. Nell told me that Bill and the gentleman driving the car did not have any injuries.

It was like a nightmare, but I did what I had to do, as I knew there were no options. I had kids to finish raising, a farm and animals to manage, with the help of the kids, family and dear friends and a full-time nursing job at the hospital.

I put on a happy face and went on with my life. At least, I tried to be happy and make my family and friends think I was coping. The network of family and friends were overwhelming and helped Lorna, J.B. and me to carry out the funeral details and get the chores done in a satisfactory manner. I could not have kept my head above water without my kids and all of the support that I received.

I made a promise to God at that time, if He and his helpers got me through the coping phrase, I would help every widow and widower in the future, and I have lived up to that promise. In fact, in doing so, I have developed a new relationship with Ella Lee Crumb which has been very rewarding to both of us. I had known Ella Lee for years but never really knew her until she lost her Dean. We are both so much alike, it scares you!

My sense of humor had to get stronger very quickly so I could hold on and survive! The old quote for whom I cannot give credit holds true, "What doesn't kill you makes you stronger!"

I had dealt with sudden death in the family before, but with a spouse it is so different. I had done a lot of death counseling both in my family and in my career. Now I was receiving counsel from everyone and very grateful.

I had always been a caretaker; it was most difficult to have to accept the help, but I did. I then learned that help is available for the asking, especially in a small rural community where we live.

There had been many deaths in our family prior to

Loren's death, and I have endured many deaths since. My father died of lung cancer when I was nineteen and in training. I thought I would die of sadness in the weeks to follow. The busy routine of learning and working kept me occupied.

My sister, Helen, the closest to my age, died when she was forty-seven of severe lung disease. Mother's death was only two years later. Before I had completely recovered from losing Mother and Helen, Loren was killed. Some days I was not sure that God understood my capabilities, but they say He never gives you more than you can handle!

Brother Clifford died several years later of lung disease after a long suffering illness. By that time brother Bob had developed lung cancer with metastasis to the bone. And people wonder why I hate tobacco products?

Bob and I had a very close relationship since we were children, and we lived only five miles apart at the time of his death. I helped transport him to and from radiation treatments and helped his wife, Laura, give him nursing care in his home.

Bob and I had a wonderful time together in his last few weeks of life. We relived our childhood experiences as we talked for hours on end. When driving him to and from the hospital, I would play old musical tapes of songs we enjoyed as young people. I had bought a new pickup truck, so I would take him on a different road each day to and from radiation to renew our old memories of the area. In my opinion, it was a wonderful way to say "good-bye!" Losing him was easy after seeing him struggle with his disease that ate his body down to skin and bones!

Renewing our childhood and talking about "Mac," as Bob called Loren, helped me to cope with losing Loren. That period, as strange as it seems, helped me to cope with Loren's sudden death and gave me the mourning period I wasn't allowed because of my responsibilities at the time.

While watching Bob die, I would sit in the swing and

look as the beautiful rose bush by the side of the porch. Laura has a "green thumb," so the roses were gorgeous in color and with many blooms. With the morning dew on the pink roses, I thought of the hymn with the words, "Dew on the roses." Some roses were dead! With meditation about Bob to God, our family and the deaths, I developed my theory about life and death, "The Rose Bush Theory." The theory is spelled out in the segment, "Life is a Choice."

15

My JOURNEY OVER THE YEARS has increased my strength, especially living with Loren and the memory of loving him. There is no doubt in my mind about that statement! Brother Bob made me tough as a child, but Loren helped me to mature into a strong woman. No doubt, God was at work over the years as He knew I would end up alone.

Surviving without Loren was hard from day one, and it has never gotten easy but with time it has become easier. As I was surviving and helping my kids to withstand the hardships without their dad, I figured out that death must be easier than bitter, tragic divorces.

Loren and I were observing a community family entering a divorce before his death. While the kids and I adjusted to living without Loren, I continued to watch that family in the community during their tragic, painful divorce which convinced me that the sorrows and loss of death can only be surpassed by the loss and sorrows of divorce. My theory being: the guilt of divorce must make it worse, as I am sure all divorced people must tell themselves, "If only!"

With Loren's death, I had no guilt; just sorrow and loss. No big money problems! Just hours of planning and management to use the insurance money correctly. No custody nightmares! No family squabbles!

I watched Lorna and her children endure a messy divorce, and that convinced me divorce is much worse and more hurtful to all concerned. Thank God, Lorna has remarried. She and Don seem to have a happy life, as happy as it can be with sharing her first four children with another family lots of the time.

Regardless of the loss, I had to survive and go on living. My method is humor, sharing it with family and having a good friend commitment. I have my good memories and my pictures, so with family and friends I still have everything. Writing this book has been therapeutic for me, and I have been able to share my good fortune, thus spreading sunshine.

Losses by death and divorce are not the only losses one has to endure during a lifetime. Aging can make losses that are difficult to accept.

With my aging body, nursing full-time as a floor duty nurse on an acute medical ward became stressful to my joints and my mind and I lost my sense of humor. I knew I had to do something different in my life to renew my humor and enjoy my remaining years with my friends and family. Loren saved the day! One night as I was walking swiftly down the hospital hall to get supplies for an emergency, I heard Loren's voice saying, "Get the Hell out of here!"

The details of my decision is spelled out in the segment. "Life is a Choice." But as I told my kids, Loren saved my neck one more time. When Loren was alive and gave stern advice, I usually took his suggestions and, thank God, I listened to his message, as he had been dead for eleven years at the time. I have never been sorry for the decision I made on the spot that night when I heard his voice!

Besides my memories of the good times, I remind myself what a smile will do for me and what a smile can do for others, so I share. A smile is another way to spread joy, as a smile is very contagious.

When I was a school nurse, I had an experience at a health screening project. I was surprised that there were so many young children who did not respond to a smile. I knew I was in the deprived area in the school district, but I did not know until that day how deprived they really were! It is hard for me to deal with people when I cannot get them to respond to my smile. To me, a smile is a good icebreaker.

As a young nurse, I was called "Sunshine" by lots of people. As I aged, I noticed I was called "Sunshine" less! At first, I thought it might be due to the gray streaks in my hair. Later I figured out that it was because of the fewer smiles.

The lack of smiles was due to the aging, squealing joints. I had to remind myself of Mr. W., an aged patient was walking down the hall holding his back one morning. I asked, "Mr. W., does your back hurt?" He smiled as he said, "Oh, honey; I have a few parts past warranty!" Now that I have parts past warranty, I have to remember to smile more. Or at least, I tried! It was a good dose of reality to see an older person with discomfort and a big smile while saying something to make others smile.

My theory which I developed over the years: my happiness is my responsibility! I try hard to work at my happiness; also I work at being healthy, as health and happiness are the two most important things to me.

I spend very little time with negative-thinking people unless I can bring a smile to their face so they will forget to be gloomy for awhile. Our surroundings do make a difference, but it is what is inside that carries us through the rough spots of life.

Music and flowers have been very important in my healing process during my life's journey. Years after Loren's death, I attended lots of musical events as I felt I could go to them alone and enjoy. I met Bob Snickles, and he was a good travel partner for over ten years before his death. We went to musical events both locally and out of state. Now I spend much of my time growing flowers for me to enjoy and share with others.

It takes most of us a lifetime to figure out what is important to us, and I was no exception. I used to think it was Loren's responsibility to provide my happiness. I had to lose him before I figured out differently.

My living process has taught me that health and happiness are the most important things in my life. Life is a three-phase process. The birthing phase is planned or not planned by our parents, the dying phase is planned by God unless we hasten our own death, the living phase is our responsibility. It only makes sense to me to be in charge of my living, as it is the only phase that I can change!

I quit working full-time to smell the roses and to survive. It worked. I have a great place in the country to do just that! Living in the country and back to nature is the place for me. I call that happiness, and it is very healthful with plenty of sunshine.

16

MY WRITING CAREER BEGAN when I quit full-time nursing and bought a word processor. I just wrote and wrote; I had heard if you want to be a writer, just write and write! So I did.

After wearing out my word processor, I bought a computer, and with trial and error I managed to rewrite my book that I wanted to share especially with my children and grandchildren as well as my friends.

I was asked to write the Harveyville News for the three local papers, *The Flint Hills Independent* and *The Osage Chronicle* in our community. Later on I wrote regularly for *The County Line* and *The Wabaunsee Signal-Enterprise*. It has been a good learning experience to express myself and share with others at the same time.

I started writing articles called "This and That" for *The Flint Hills Independent,* and the subject would be anything that "turned me on," which covered quite a large territory. I really wanted to become Erma Brombeck of the Flints Hills, but that never happened. It depends who you talk with about how close I came!

My writing evidently spread out to other papers, so I will include a sample of some of the published articles.

"Hard Work Pays Off" was published in *Celebrating the Century*, a book of essays written by Kansans and published in The *Topeka Capital-Journal* 1999-2000. Celebrate 2000, envision the future.

My long-range plan was to go to nurse's training after high school, but first I needed dentures at the tender age of 16. I needed money to pay for the dentures before going to college for my nursing education.

I started working at the Purple Cow, the coffee shop in the Hotel Kansan at 9th and Kansas Avenue as a waitress. The tips I made during the summer months of 1953 paid for my teeth. It was a good thing the tips were good because the salary was very low. This was back when the downtown area was the only shopping area in town.

I stayed with my sister, Bessie Eastman, who lived in Topeka. In the 1950s no one commuted to and from Topeka on a daily basis from my hometown of Eskridge. Bessie lived in the vicinity of 6th and Madison. When I walked home after 11 p.m., no one bothered me. There is a grave difference in walking after dark today.

Walking was the only way to get around, as Bessie did not have a car and the buses did not run after 10 p.m.

During the summer of 1954 I again worked at the Purple Cow, and my best friend, Carol Weekes Swenson, joined me in making money for our first year of college. The work was hard, especially the year of the Topeka Centennial. We served lots of nice people, and the tips were great. Some gave a little more when they learned we were headed for college.

I value all of my experience, starting with my first job at the Purple Cow.

****

"Starched Memories" was published in the *Star Magazine* of the *Kansas City Star* in the section of "Remember When" on July 27, 1997.

I took nurse's training in Kansas City, before hospitals had central air conditioning and the summers were sweltering. Back in those days, nurses wore white cotton dress uni-

forms with heavy starch, including a cap and white hose. Can you picture what the uniform looked like after an hour or two of work? I can still feel the soggy cotton belt around my waist and the extreme discomfort that I felt each hot summer day.

I was a chubby little farm gal, and starched uniforms were a source of irritation to me, without the added heat and sweat. I was used to good country air and a gentle breeze quite often. The hospital just had hot air and lots of sweat without a break under shade trees. I longed for a sweet-smelling country breeze to cool my brow.

I realized the lack of air conditioning was only part of my distress. I longed to be out in the country. Cool, comfortable air could made both my patients and me feel better.

I was not the only one who was uncomfortable; the patients were very ill and looked miserable, with or without a fever! Many complications were added to their illness due to lack of proper room ventilation and heat control.

My memories of working in the garden and cutting sunflowers on the farm gave me mental relief as I would dream of the shady places and the cool drinks of well water.

My sister, Helen, resided in Kansas City and was raising her babies during that period. Their apartment was upstairs and very hot. Helen would set a dish pan of water at the foot of the bed in front of an electric fan so the children could take a nap in the heat of the day. Her husband, Carl, would take them for an evening ride to cool off before going to bed. Some evenings I was invited to ride along, and what a nice relief!

In the hospital we used lots of soothing wet cloths to sponge off the sick people as we provided them with extra fluids. I do not remember any hospital fans; opened windows were the only cooling system available.

I was very lucky; I had an electric fan for my sleeping room, thanks to my sister, Bessie. My classmates did not have any fans, so they napped on my bed when I was working.

Now, 40 years later, I have central air and heat in my country home, but my vivid memories remind me of the times when lots of people did not have comfort as we do today.

****

"Outhouses to Outer Space" was published in *The Flint Hills Independent* on September 19, 1996.

My age of people and older have lived through many changes in society from outhouses to outer space with lots of big changes in between. I cannot help but wonder what my children and grandchildren will see in the next 50 years and how it will compare to what I have witnessed.

My dad, Fred Eastman, died in 1955, but I wish it were possible to speak with him about life today and how he would compare it with the life in his youth. My desire to hear what he would have to say about the changes in society from 1955 to 1996 is even greater. He had a great sense of humor, and I do believe he could put some real funny angles in his comparison.

My interest in changes that have occurred is greater since starting my research for my writing about life in yesteryear. I have interviewed many people and have written from their viewpoints for a family project. The term, outhouses to outer space, caught my eye in a research book that was loaned to me for that project. That phrase really got me to thinking.

My friends have made many comments about my writing on bathrooms, and little did they know what was in store! I have never even touched on outhouses until now, and that is a subject where lots can be said! However, I think I will pass on that one, Sears Catalogs are scarce! The modern term, "Porta Potty," keeps all of us humble when we attend fairs and other outdoor events. Can you imagine using one, day and night, in all kinds of weather?

Enough said! I am going to spare you about outer space,

as I know nothing about it and do not care to research the subject. I just know the human race has discovered many new wonders in the past 50 years that I have been watching. The first 10 years of my life was spent carrying some water, milk and wood to the house and chopping weeds, when I was not riding the horse to carry water to the men in the field.

When the first man walked on the moon, Loren Masters threatened me that he and Tony Young were going to get the first hay hauling contract on the moon, but I told him to count me out as I was not leaving solid ground to work. Besides, I had always been told there was only green cheese up there. No mention of hay before or after the moon walk!

Modern bathrooms bring us much comfort, and technology brings us many pleasures and facts through satellites in outer space. I am happy to say that I have enjoyed the comfort with that improvement. It was nice to watch the developments.

****

"What Germs?" was published in *The Flint Hills Independent* on January 11, 1996.

Have you ever noticed that food servers wear plastic gloves, but the same gloved hand accepts your payment? I find this most amusing until the heavy cold and flu season is in progress.

I am not fond of germs, but I do know they are everywhere! I remember when we all drank water out of the same dipper. Success and progress afforded us individual cups. After society became aware of improved sanitation practices, someone promoted chip-and-dip bowls. Sure enough, we all are back to eating out of the same bowl! Not much different than the "same old dipper" method! Oh, I know I am not supposed to put the same chip in the dip twice, but watch those around you at a party!

By the time we all became lovers of chips and dip, some-one designed the salad bar. Talk about cross-contamination! Never sit close enough to the bar that you can observe others or your appetite will wither. Don't get me wrong, I love salad bars, but I certainly do not sit in view of the bar. I used to — but my observation skills were ruining my eating out.

Recent top news stories were about hand-washing tech-niques in the hospital setting. Believe me, my keen observa-tions started in hospitals, and now C.B.S. News is making you aware of human error where risks are high. If I recited all of my experiences, this article would lose the humor angle.

Poor hand-washing practices are seen everywhere! Just watch the people ahead of you in a public restroom, espe-cially waitresses and patrons in restaurants. Think about it — even some of the fussy-dressed folks bypass the sink.

Back to the gloved hand, let's talk about federal policy. I worked in a federal hospital at the time the of federal man-date for wearing plastic gloves when handling any body waste. Our unit was out of gloves before the end of the first week. That is called progress? Personally, I would have saved some of the gloves for the real messy cleanups! Gloves are only a cover-up unless you use good planning and natural brain power.

I must give those federal people a break, as many of the same people are not getting paid as of now. And that is not funny!

Nothing beats good hand washing regardless of your occupation or doing the fun times. Many people never out-grow what I call the "little boy washing technique," which is just getting close to the tap water and ignoring the soap!

****

"City Pasture" was published in *The Wabaunsee County Signal-Enterprise* in the "This and That" column on April 13, 2000.

I wrote a memory of Eskridge when asked to write a special memory to be put in the new Wabaunsee County history book, "Stories from the Past," 3rd edition. So I wanted to share it with you in anticipation of the arrival of the new book.

In the 1990s milking your own cows for milk to drink is a lost art. If you remember, during the 1940s and before, many people, including town folks, milked their own cow for the daily supply of milk and cream. Some of the town people sold raw milk to others living in town who did not own their cow.

In Eskridge, Kansas, during the early years, there was always a "city pasture" where town people kept their cows. The pasture that I remember was just south of town on the west side of old #4 Highway. Remember, we are speaking about the 1940s when the highway went south of town one mile and then west.

I learned from Mrs. Norma Akers Corpening that the "city pasture" was owned by Mr. Elwood Parsonage from Topeka and was rented out to citizens in town. Later Russell Taylor bought the pasture from relatives after Mr. Parsonage's death in 1964.

Early each day people walked out to the pasture and milked their cow out in the open at the corner of the pasture. Then they carried the milk home and returned in the late afternoon to do it again. I never learned where the people kept their milk stools and "kickers," a metal device that fits around the hind legs on the hocks to keep the cow from kicking while being milked. Think of milking in the open air in all kinds of weather, rain or shine, to say nothing of cold, snowy days!

The out-of-doors procedure caught my eye because we always had a milk barn to milk our cows ever since I can remember. Our barn stored the cream separator and other necessary items for milking, such as "kickers" and stools. My family, the Fred Eastman family, lived on the Hentzler farm south of town, so we passed the town pasture quite often at milking time.

Frank Cooper shared his memories of his cow milking days while living in town, and they pastured their cows in another pasture on the east side of Eskridge behind the Baptist Church which was owned by Dr. Stewart, who charged monthly rent for each cow. Frank said some of the people who rented space in the Stewart pasture walked their cows to the Parmeter barn to milk them and leave them overnight.

Life in Eskridge or anyplace has greatly changed since then. Many kids do not know from where milk comes. Very few farm people milk cows for their own use today. Our milk comes from large dairies, pasteurized and shipped to the grocery stores. Lots has changed in our way of living, to say nothing of our cholesterol levels. If we still milked our cows at the town pasture, can you imagine how many trucks would be parked there? Have we gotten soft?

****

"Morning Tranquillity" was published in *The County Line* as Dorothy's Thoughts on June 16, 1999.

As I awaken in the early morning, I hear only the birds singing a pleasant wake-up tune. I live in a quiet country home; there is no need for heavy drapes and closed shutters to shut out noise for good sleeping. No noisy neighbors or busy byways. Windows are left open for welcomed country air and good smells of nature. This is as close to Heaven as I can get while still on earth!

The warm morning light helps me to open my eyes to the wonders of nature around me. I thank God for the pleasure of living one more day in the midst of this underlying beauty. The beauty changes from day to day, always something to look at and admire on the trail of life. I am grateful to live in a free country with clean air to breathe and clear water to drink, as they are my greatest needs.

After a quiet breakfast with the morning paper, I climb on my all-terrain vehicle and scout the brome fields and pasture for unwanted thistles. There is perfect tranquillity while searching for noxious weeds. How can anything be so pretty and yet so noxious? It is illegal to let the blooms grow and spread. Only the weeds are unwanted, as all of the other elements are delightful.

Destroying thistles is work, but with the quiet peaceful morning sunrise it is enjoyable to me. Working while watching the sunrise mixes pleasure with work. I cannot keep from admiring the beautiful bloom of the musk thistles as I destroy them. It is hard to destroy a gorgeous bloom that has hundreds of wavy hairs that glisten in the morning sun with the dew heavy on the plant.

I cannot help thinking about the hours of toil in my yard just to produce pretty blooms, and now I am destroying God's art. But I know there will be a fine to pay if the noxious weeds take over my property. Besides, cattle do not eat thistles!

There are many other distractions while working, such as quacking ducks flying overhead going to the next pond. The bumblebees are humming about the blooms, praying I will miss some of them. A bobwhite quail makes a clear whistling call as the low hum of my three-wheeler was drowned out by the low-flying small airplane checking the power lines in the north pasture.

Both of my containers are full of snipped blooms and the sprayer was out of 24D, so it was time to go to the house and wait until evening to scout for more musk thistles. Morning tranquillity was over, but there will be a gorgeous sunset this evening, and I can accomplish more work as I enjoy the nature around me.

****

Part II

FUN ON THE RUN

DEDICATION

To my loved ones, to whom I feel compelled to record my experiences. My dear husband, Loren Masters, was killed before our children were mature. Therefore, the grandchildren never had the pleasure of knowing him.

I lost my father, Fred Eastman, while I was a student in nursing. I know what my children have missed by not knowing their dad from the eyes of an adult.

I want my family to know more about Loren and the Eastman family, if only through my eyes.

Love,
Dorothy M. Eastman Masters

March 18, 1998

17

I HAVE HAD A GOOD LIFE, and from being born in 1936 after the Great Depression to a farm family with six other kids, that alone is a miracle.

My dad, Fred Lorenza Eastman, had a good sense of humor, but I am sure it got warped considerably trying to feed another mouth. Maybe the name, Lorenza, that he was given by his parents created his need for humor. A way to survive!

My mother, Golden Myrtle McMaster, also had reason to be able to laugh at herself and those around her with a name like Myrtle, to say nothing of Golden. Most people insisted her name was Goldie. She held to the name her parents gave her and corrected people when the exact name was important.

My ability to laugh easily probably occurred during my first summer, as the heat was high and dry and the dust storms were difficult for everyone. The grasshoppers moved into the Kansas Flint Hills where my family farmed and raised livestock.

A baby smiling and laughing more than likely was God's work shining through in a mysterious way.

I never questioned their love for me because they took care of me in spite of all their hardships. I had six older siblings to help me find humor and love in the world around me.

This is not your ordinary autobiography. The only outstanding thing about my life was the different experiences and the amount of fun I have found along life's journey.

The following pages will be numerous episodes of having fun on the run through life. They will not connect to make a story. My lifeline is the only string that ties the episodes together.

I bought a computer to complete this mission, and the following episode unraveled when I was reading this morning's paper and spied an obituary.

Malcomn McHenry, Jr. was a veteran at the Colmery O'Neil Veterans Hospital in Topeka, Kansas, and both Loren and I cared for him at different points in our career at the V.A. He had lost an arm before he made the art for Loren. His obituary was in today's (2/26/1998) paper and stimulated this memory. He was a poet and painter, as well as a farmer and rancher. He also was a car salesman at one point in his lifetime.

All of the above occupations made him interesting to Loren and me. I closed my eyes after reading his obituary and could see Loren and Mr. McHenry giving each other a bad time on the ward. Loren had a unique manner of evaluating his patients, family and friends' abilities, to encourage their best qualities. Now Mr. McHenry and Loren can visit in Heaven and watch over us as we travel through our life's journey.

The painting over our bed was done by Mr. McHenry. Loren liked the painting so well, I had John Cary Jr., the Burlingame mortician, frame it for Loren for Christmas. That was before I had met and cared for Mr. McHenry.

I met Mr. McHenry as a patient on Ward I-4A after John Cary had buried Loren. God has some strange ways of connecting people. I met lots of patients on I-4A that I recognized from Loren's description of the person's talent and behavior.

The picture of a Roman athlete running with a javelin tooled on bronze that hangs in the kitchen was given to Loren many years ago. Loren liked the art work and had

Mr. McHenry mount it on a piece of old barn board. The board was from the barn we helped Loren tear down at Gladys Peart's farm. Lorna and J.B., do you remember the Sunday when Herb, Mary Lou and Roger Anderson helped us to demolish that barn? We had a picnic and salvaged pieces of barn siding to save memories and pieces of art work in the future.

Your dad had extra fond memories of the barn, as he had lived on that farm with his family from 1947 to 1960. They were living there when Loren and I started dating. The farm has history related to the City of Harveyville. Our town was named after the Harvey Family that owned the farm at the time the first post office was built there in a log cabin. Remains of the log cabin were there in 1958 when I first visited that farm. Bette Watson and I went to buy fresh farm eggs. The real truth, Bette was playing cupid! Whatever, it worked, as I married Loren two years later.

****

J.B. and Dr. William Harold Walker of Eskridge, Kansas, when J.B. had his first genital exam:

"Why, Doctor Walker!" exclaimed J.B. as the doctor checked his testicles to see if they had descended properly. When Dr. Walker did the rectal exam, J.B. put his hands on his hips and turned to see the doctor as he said emphatically, "Well, Doctor Walker!"

J.B. has water-clear, beautiful blue eyes and he knew just how to use them. His eyes grew in size as he scolded the doctor.

Doctor Walker smiled but said nothing. I never said anything at the time and later tried to explain to J.B. why the doctor could touch his private parts but not other people. That is a hard lesson to teach. I can only imagine how hard it is for the small child to learn, when it is years later before they understand the lesson . It is impossible to alert small children to every detail the doctor may do to them in the act of helping them.

****

Lorna was embarrassed when Dr. Sherwood examined her for her first hernia repair at the young age of five. She was lying on his examining table; Doc would pull her panties down to her pubic area and she would pull them up. He peered over his half glasses and said to me, "Mother, you have taught her well!" as he smiled. I explained to her that the doctor had to feel her hernia. So she allowed him to do so. He had to see it and feel it before setting her up for surgery.

****

Before adopting our children, I became aware of the need to help children understand medical and nursing practices without scaring them before the exam. As a nurse of many years, I had observed children who were frightened at the sight of me and other nurses in full uniform. I had seen the effects of people scaring children with threats of what a doctor or nurse would do to them.

In the 1960s I worked in the clinic and emergency room at the Santa Fe Hospital in Topeka, Kansas. The clinic was right inside the back door and children would scream at the sight of me in uniform. It had to be the uniform and possible threats, as my appearance did not make children scream when I was dressed in street clothes.

I would hear people who did not know how to properly discipline their children scare them with the statement, "The nurse will give you a shot if you do not stop misbehaving!" Can you imagine where I would have liked to put the needle?"

****

My oldest sister, Bessie, was a real character, and evidently she got her terrific personality from her middle name when she was born in 1919 and given the name Bessie Myrtle Eastman. Is that a handle or not? She was the first born and was the lucky one to get Momma's name!

She needed humor, as she had to help raise the next six

kids. She had a tender spot in her heart for all of us until the day she died at age 74.

Bessie started to work outside our home at an early age, after quitting high school to make her own living. Times were hard in the 1930s; many people her age did not complete school,

I do not remember living with her until I stayed at her apartment when I started working away from home prior to going to nurse's training.

Bessie never married, so her nieces and nephews were treated by her as her very own. She was very bossy, but it was because she was so protective. It was her way of showing her love and need to receive love. She had to appear tough to survive.

Throughout this book as the funny things strike my memory, you will read about Bessie's humor.

She would give you the shirt off of her back and then give you Hell like she didn't like you. But you knew better, because she would be there the next time you needed a helping hand. Of course, there were people who did not give her the second chance, and that was their loss.

Bessie moved to Harveyville in 1981 so she would be close, so Loren and I could help her as she aged more. Little did we know she would outlive Loren by eleven years.

****

Bette Watson was the first registered nurse with whom I developed a close relationship when I began working at the V. A. Hospital. As I mentioned earlier in the book, she was a real pal in convincing Loren I was the gal for him. He moved so slowly in the courting phase, I was not sure he was interested in anything except just teasing me. He had lots of help in that department.

Bill Johnson was his best helper, both with the patients on the ward as well as how to chase me and drive me crazy in love with Loren, all at the same time. Bill was also an aide on the ward, and he and Loren were the two most caring men I had ever worked with in a nursing setting. They were terrific with the patients and each other, as well as most of the employees. After I joined the ranks on that ward, I was included on their team. Bette and Leah had been on their team for a long time.

Leah Hefner was a registered nurse and a great cupid as well. She impressed upon Loren over the months that I was worthy of his attention. But he still courted slowly. I was a registered nurse, and the nurses were his supervisor for the ward routines. Men do not like women as their boss; therefore it hampered the dating scene.

I changed jobs when an inter-ward transfer was not allowed as I requested. I did not like working at the V.A., so I left and started working at the Santa Fe Hospital. Our romance picked up after I was no longer the boss on the job, so to speak!

Changing jobs may appear severe, as a large decrease in salary and some loss of benefits occurred. This was in the 1950s, and the work place was different than in the present. Nurses dating their aides was prohibited, so the ball was in my court. I did not tell my supervisor why I wanted a transfer, and it was not granted.

Life is a choice, and I chose to make less money at the time, and my income today reflects that career move, but I have my pride and it is worth more than money to me. Money does not buy health and it does not buy happiness. However, pride will carry you for a lifetime.

The Santa Fe Hospital, which later became the Memorial Hospital, was the best place I ever worked. In fact, this Saturday I will attend a wedding of a friend, Margaret DeWitt, that I met there in 1959. Margaret was one of my supervisors. At the Santa Fe Hospital the patients and employees, including the doctors, were one big happy family, and that does not happen everywhere.

I still maintain a close relationship with Bill Johnson, Leah Hefner, Walter Mullens, Bette Watson and Margaret

DeWitt, soon to be Margaret Sayler, to name a few.

Joining the staff at the Santa Fe Hospital changed my world completely. Bigger and better things than money occurred during this employment. Loren asked me to marry him. My first supervisor, Maxine Swalwell Craig, was instrumental in allowing us to adopt our first child, Lorna Mae Masters Lister Lawton.

Talk about benefits! There are no work benefits that compare to family love, and winning love from the best man in the world, Loren Bryan Masters. Loren and I got married on May 21, 1960, and we continued to work at the different hospitals. Life was good!

Loren and I had a fun time doing our jobs at the hospitals and working on the farm. But best of all was having each other to enjoy while we worked and played. Between the two of us, more family and friends were available for more enjoyment.

After three years of married life and one miscarriage, Maxine Craig called me to see if we would like to adopt a baby! What a question! Loren and I were thrilled beyond words. Both of us wanted a family as much as we wanted our life together to continue.

Maxine had quit working for the hospital and went to work for a obstetrician, which was a blessing for us. The hand of God, Maxine and the doctor placed a cute little bundle in our arms. What fun we had with our little baby girl, Lorna Mae. She was the first adopted child in either family, but not the last!

Now life was really good, and soon we started looking for a little boy. Thanks to God and the Kansas Children's Service League, we had the pleasure of adopting James Bryan. Loren wanted to name his Jim after his deceased brother which was fine with me. But I wanted to call him J.B. so people would not say Jim Who? There were so many people named Jim.

His name, J.B., was jokingly changed to P.J. as is Family

Circus, or B.J. But he will always be J.B. to me. His aunts call him James Bryan just like so many people refer to Loren as Loren Bryan. The name Bryan came from Loren's dad, Bryan George Masters.

Now our family was complete!

****

When I first met Loren, the Veteran's Hospital was housed in the old buildings that had been Winter General Hospital during the wartime. The buildings were long barracks that had about 25 patients per building.

My first experience was on a three-ward unit in the B building. B-6 was a nightmare for a young nurse directly from a training hospital. The majority of the patients had psychiatric problems, and many of them were quite senile. I will spare you the details, but I must say Loren and his buddies (aides) loved to observe the shocked look on the new young nurse's face.

My psychiatric experience was limited to a three-month training session in a private psychiatric hospital. There were a big difference in a private hospital and a veteran's psychiatric ward. The time was 1957 and tranquilizers were new on the market, and the regulation of psychiatric medicines are trial and error. The mental problems had a head start on the treatment plan. Men, muscle and restraint were necessary.

I was totally shocked at the sight of most of the patients on 6-B. Loren and his pals were shocked at first, but they were used to the sights by the time I joined the staff. With my mouth dropped open and a strange look on my face, I gave them plenty to enjoy. Quickly, they educated me about caring for old men, and drapes or modesty were not part of the education. But they cared for them and provided the best quality of life available for their present mental and physical conditions.

Loren was called "Mac" by his co-workers, and the nickname made him even cuter in my eyes. He had a chubby face with a boyish grin and a cute little wink that curled my ears. By the time the shock wore off, the flirtation began.

Loren had been living with his parents in rural Harveyville since he got out of the Army. He move to Topeka with me when we got married. He then drove to the farm on his days off to do the farming.

We rented our first house from "Chubb" and "Boots" Meisenheimer on the Quail Farm which was an old polo farm on 49th Street, southwest of Topeka. They were great landlords and treated us as if we were their own children. They told us they would not complain if we had late parties if we did not complain when they had late parties. It was a deal! We had a great time during the four years at that location.

We had our horse there so we could ride in the evenings, and Loren enjoyed that as he got off three hours earlier than I did. He did lots of odd jobs like trimming trees and grass for Chubb. Boots hated it when they trimmed the trees. Loren was uncomfortable when up in a tree, and she would drive in and give Chubb a piece of her mind. Loren would just hide between the branches until she went into the house.

Loren got to ride his first riding lawn mower, as the Meisenheimers owned the Shawnee Ford Tractor Company where "Chubb" spent most of his time. In 1960, the riding mowers were considerably smaller than they are today. You are going to have to fill the spaces of his description of how he felt he look. He told me, "When I ride that little mower, I bet I look like a monkey _ _ _ _ _ _ _ a football." Remember back, Loren was short and chubby, and the riding mower was so small!

****

Yesterday I saw Edith Kuhn, and she was at the wedding of my nurse friend, Margaret, from Santa Fe Hospital. I have only seen Edith a few times since I left the V.A. Hospital in 1959. She was and is a loyal supporter of Loren Masters. She promised me she would come to lunch at the Harveyville Cafe soon with Florence Waters so we could

137

reminisce about the life and times on the old V.A. ward with the antics of Loren as our lunch topic.

Edith thought my writing about Loren for a legacy for my children was a great idea, and she will add memories. Both Edith and Florence were seasoned registered nurses when I got to V.A. and met Loren. They taught me professional tricks on the ward, while Loren and his crew taught me practical ways to accomplish the same goal.

Every day I am amazed of how God works in mysterious ways in connecting people and reconnecting us as we grow in the workplace which continues into maturity.

****

Bette Watson who now lives in Montana writes me her memories of Loren. "Loren was on time, friendly, looking neat as a pin, full of laughs and a real co-worker. He, Sam Smith, Bill Johnson made my evening shift! One Halloween they thought it would be great to have a meal with each of us bringing something. Bill Johnson brought jalapeno peppers, which I had never tried."

"At the time I was pregnant and thought they were like pickles. Well, needless to say, they were just a tad (A WHOLE LOT) hotter — and Mike churned for three days (inutero) while my mouth burned. The guys laughed until they were numb."

Bette Watson added, "We always got our work done and then played. One time when a mental patient called me a whore as we were putting him in restraints. I replied, "What I do off duty is my own business!"

Bette admitted that after the patient was secured, Loren and Sam informed Bette to never let her respect down again. In those days, respect meant everything, and the aides were more than supportive to the nurses. I am just guessing, but I bet that was the last time Bette made that remark. The incident has stayed on her mind for forty years.

****

I worked and enjoyed the fellows and fell madly in love

138

with Loren and decided to change jobs and see if our love would develop into a permanent relationship. I had worked on the afternoon shift with Bette and Loren for the past year while I took morning courses at Washburn University. The employee togetherness was outstanding. Most of the nurses knew Loren and I went places together after our tour of duty.

When Bette found I had written a resignation, she wrote out a two-week notice also. I could not believe my ears when I learned she had also resigned. Her reply was, "Now they can hire two new nurses and I will stay home and raise my son, Mike!"

Another one of Loren's fun pals was John Jackson, and their antics together was clever to me. John had so much physical agility and Loren had so much physical stamina. There wasn't anything they could not accomplish together, especially with Sam Smith and Bill Johnson's help.

****

Loren was just as much fun on the farm, and his work ethic was the same as at the hospital. Get the work done and done right with some fun along the way, and after the work is completed, more fun.

Loren and his parents, Bryan and Mae, had bought the farm on the hill just before we were married. Besides that 80 acres, they rented farm and pasture land. He was a busy boy. Dad Masters had his cancerous lung removed before I met him and was semi-retired. Mom Masters was a regular right-hand man; in fact, she loved outdoor work better than house work.

When Mom left the field, she would whip up a fine meal. I can still taste some of her good dishes. Lorna learned to cook, Grandma Style. Mom would let her throw more flour about the kitchen than I would allow her to do. So it was much more fun to cook at Grandma's house.

J.B. liked the house rules at Grandpa's better than he did at home. Grandpa would let him eat the cake frosting and then leave the cake because, "It was too sweet!"

****

When Lorna was one year old, we left the Quail Farm and moved further south and west of Topeka to the Engler rental house on Crooked Post Road, which is named 57th Street today.

That location was nice but it was bad luck for us, as crooks stole our new furniture and many of our belongings as soon as we were settled in and comfortable.

A year later that house was severely damaged by the 1966 tornado. Thank God, Loren and Lorna went to Burlingame to his sister's house where I was selling Tupperware, as the tornado moved through that area by the time we reached Burlingame.

Then we moved to the Harveyville area. We stayed in a farmhouse north of town until we could find a better place. We lived a year in the green rental house of Harold and Hazel Von Rohr in Harveyville.

J.B. came to make his home with us while living in Harveyville. We soon outgrew that house, just as we did our first small home after Lorna came to live with us.

Loren and I had bought our farm, Mortgage Ridge, when Lorna was a baby. We decided it was time for us to build a home on the property and live in the country where we both wanted to live.

We had plans to build a home and "chickened out" because of finances. We bought a new mobile home and had it set on our farm. We moved into the trailer in November 1967. All of us like living in the country with fresh air and freedom.

Loren and I both liked kids, and we adored our little children. Lorna and J.B. made all of our hard work seem very worthwhile. We enjoyed seeing them grow and learn new things.

Loren and his teasing ways continued with our kids and Toni Eastman, my brother, Bob's girl. Bob Eastman and I had been very close when growing up both in age and interests, and that continued after I was married until Bob died in 1988.

****

Now, about me! This book is about my fun on the run, and you have met the most important characters, Loren and our kids, Lorna and J.B., who got involved in my fun run when I started adulthood.

I have had a good life, not always easy, but no one in my early childhood told me it would be easy. Watching my family make a living and learning to help was all I needed to know about working and having fun at the same time.

No one that I know has had an easy life if they are productive citizens. Working for a living can be difficult, but it can also be fun during the process with the right kind of people around you.

The best luck I have ever had was my family taught me how to work inside and outdoors! Later Loren showed me his tricks of the trade, and I knew I was wealthy because of my relationships with people.

Hardships come to everyone, some just more than others. All of us have the choice, to work through the bumps of life or let them keep us in a rut. My choice was to get up, dust off my bitches and travel on.

The late Bob Eastman was my favorite brother as he was the closest to my age, two and one-half years older than I. He was the main character in my fun on the run as a child.

With Bob and me, the fun was on the back of a horse. We would have the horse on dead run if out of the sight of our dad. We like to ride like the wind and we got into "thunder" with our dad more than once for wild rides.

One evening Bob and I went to the pasture to get the riding horse and we had one bridle. Bob had a colt in the same pasture, so he decided to use the bridle for the colt and that left nothing for me to use on the big tame horse named Dan.

We did not think I would get myself or the horse into any problems, but we played in the pasture too long. When darkness overtook us, we decided to hit the trail for the house. The pasture was across the country road from the house and barn. Bob was a great one to make a bet on the race to the barn. We had left the gate open and did not realize our dad had closed the gate to the pasture.

Bob set the rules for the race. Keep in mind, I do not have a thing in which to control my horse should something go wrong! Bob said, "When we get to the top of the hill, we will be able to see if any cars are coming down the road; if not, kick old Dan and I will race you to the barn!"

It sounded like a fun race to me, so I followed his suggestion. Dan was tall and fast, and I knew I could beat Bob and his small colt. No cars in sight, so I kick my horse and said, "Let's go, Dan!"

By the time Dan and I could see that the gate had been closed, it was too late to stop. You guessed it — Dan started to jump the gate as Bob had taught him well about jumping. I was sitting up there with the wind in my face, a prayer in my heart and a lump in throat.

Dan got his hind leg caught in the fence and was floundering around; I started to jump off of his back. Dad was running to the gate with wire pliers in hand as he had heard the thundering hoofs.

My dad's voice said, "Dorf, sit on that horse and ride him. As you got in that mess, you ride him until he gets out." So I did; after all, Dad was holding the weapon (wire pliers). I do not recall ever doing that again, but I never forgot that race.

As you know by now, my quick name or kick name was "Dorf." Thank God, it did not stick for life. Bob started it, and it went to the grave with him as I do not recall being called "Dorf" since.

Besides Bob, my sister, Helen, was at home for part of my childhood. She was seven years and seven days older than I. She was an interesting and fun sister.

Helen was a typical bigger sister, and she did the "big sister things" for me like fix my hair and play school and dolls with me when I was little.

Fun with Helen continued when I was in nurse's training at the hospital in Kansas City as she and her family lived there.

Elizabeth "Liz" Eastman Mercer was the next sister, and she was eleven years older than I. She started her family when I was little, and her oldest girl, Betty, was only six years younger than I. Liz's husband at the time was named Keith, and while he was in the Army, Liz and her family lived with us on the farm. So we were very close, and my little nieces and nephews played with me like brothers and sisters during that time.

After Keith got out of the Army, Liz and her family moved to Burlingame. I would ride "Old Polly," the Santa Fe train from Eskridge through Harveyville to Burlingame, to visit Liz and her family. I had many fun times playing with her and her family.

When I attended rural school, District #20, I was the only child in grades one through three. The older children pampered me and protected me.

I started town school in Eskridge in the fourth grade, and a lifetime friendship developed with Carol Weekes Swenson and the real fun began. To this day, we call, write each other and tape messages on a weekly basis. We have suffered through many battles and have won, as we are still friends today. That's love and devotion.

****

My oldest brother was Clifford Lorenza. That's right, he was saddled with Dad's middle name. A name I have not heard anywhere else and, believe me, it was not spoken too many times around our house.

Cliff had beautiful, water-clear blue eyes, and his sense of humor matched his eyes. When I was young, I would hear my Mother say, "You can find Clifford where the women are!" I never saw him in that light until later in life. He had many cute little sayings with his eyes just snapping.

Clifford was the "money man" in our family; he talked money, he dreamed money and it gave his pretty blue eyes a green hue.

Of course, Clifford remembered the Great Depression, and it left a great impact on his thinking. I was lucky enough to be born at the end of the depression.

Joseph Raymond Eastman, as he was named, called himself Jack. Mother said he gave himself the name as a small child and it stuck until he entered the Navy. Jack was a good-looking guy in his uniform and the only member of my immediate family that was in the Armed Forces. It was so sad to see him leave for war, just as it was for all the service men in World War II.

Later Jack became J.R., before the Dallas television series. J.R. really fits his personality.

****

So much for the basis of my childhood and my family at this point. I chose to write this book so my children and their children would know Loren B. Masters through my eyes and the eyes of his dear friends who knew him well. He was a terrific fellow and well loved, and his grandchildren deserve to know that!

Since my dad died when I was nineteen, I feel the need to leave a legacy for my family about Loren and some facts about my family that died before my kids were very old and before I had grandchildren. History is gone if not preserved in writing for future generations.

Loren had the opportunity to meet my dad, Fred Eastman, while Loren was working for the Wabaunsee County. He and his co-workers hauled rocks out of our pasture for the county roads.

I did not meet Loren at that time, but he later teased me, saying that he knew me from watching me riding the horse across the fields and pasture. I never bought that idea of acquaintance! I met him at the V.A. Hospital when I was a scared new registered nurse in an entirely different setting from anything I had ever set foot into before!

When Loren first told me that he knew me from riding my horse across the pasture, I had no idea what he was referring to, and he took his own sweet time explaining his statement to me. Loren had an answer for everything with a wink in his eye, especially if he was trying to out-best someone.

****

Many people have jogged my memory of Loren and his great personality since they have heard about me writing this book. His friends and mine have been very attentive over the past sixteen years since Loren's accidental death.

Loren and J.B. went hunting in western Kansas very year with Ira Austin, his boys and other guys such as Steve Clark. Ira filled up the station wagon and headed towards Linn, Kansas, every fall.

To quote Steve Clark, "Loren had a big heart in a big body. What he lacked in speed when we were hunting together, he made up for in determination. When we both ran after crippled pheasants, Bob Austin said it sounded like thundering hoofs!"

"Loren loved to attend the kids' activities. Lorna was his late-life little sweetie pie, and his eyes showed true love when she was with him. Loren would bust the buttons off of his shirt with pride as he watched J.B. play sports!" added Steve.

I watched Loren as he watched his kids in different events, and Steve said it best! Loren loved kids, and he insisted that they behave while having a good time; that way all of us had a better time. Loren was loyal to the entire team, and the kids knew Loren expected their best each game.

The boys on J.B.'s basketball team must have felt the love Loren showed for them as they dedicated their first

145

place trophy in his honor at the first tournament after his death. J.B. got to receive the trophy for his dad at Osage, and he accepted the trophy like a man. J.B. was only 15 years old. That had to be hard for a young lad, but he did what he had to do, to carry on through life, just as his dad expected him to do.

****

Loren's duties as a psychiatric aide had increased, and he was expected to do more charting after we were married in 1960. Loren was a smart man with lots of common sense, but he "would go to pieces" with paper and pen. He could perform any duty explained well to him, but to evaluate it on paper was another thing. He would ask me to help him write his notes at home, and then he would transfer the notes on the patients' charts the next day at the hospital.

I would try to get him to use the dictionary so as to become more self-sufficient and increase his self-worth, as he was very capable, just scared of his ability with a pen and paper.

His words back to me, "The dictionary is no good to me as I cannot spell! If I could spell, I wouldn't need a dictionary!" He believed that with all of his heart, and I continued to help him at home. It was so little to do, to help just a good guy who helped so many people in so many ways.

****

From 1960 to 1966 Loren and I lived to two small houses in the outskirts of Topeka, the first place being the Quail Farm and the second the small house that was hit by the 1966 tornado. We moved out of it during the night after the storm, as we decided not to stay there while the owner repaired the house.

We felt the place was jinxed for us as we had been robbed of our new furniture and belongings the previous year. Two disasters in two years was a strong indication for us to move on. Besides, Loren loved his farming, and it made sense to move closer to the farm and drive to the city to work.

146

After renting the VonRohr House in Harveyville, we bought a mobile home for our farm. Then we were where we wanted to be and were a happy foursome.

Loren named our place Mortgage Ridge. We never changed the name after the mortgage was paid off. We later re-mortgaged to buy more land; the name stays, with or without a mortgage.

J.B. was one year old when we moved to Mortgage Ridge, and Lorna was four. Living in the country was where Loren and I wanted to live and to raise our family. Our kids liked the nature around them and still prefer country living. The birds, frogs and deer provide much entertainment.

J.B. was happy that he could run across the pasture behind our house to fish. Our pond was close to the house, within shouting distance. He now says I made him run up on top of the dam so often so I could see he was all right that he never had time to fish. However, he carried many nice bass home, and I have pictures to prove my story.

J.B. made his own entertainment at the creek, running his home-made traps and other little boy games.

Our farm was just like Old McDonald's Farm at one time. Every time we had company, the kids dragged all of them to see their rabbits, Golden Pheasant, pigs, horses and cattle. Thanks to the pigs, the turkeys never lived long enough to be shown.

Loren had an old bathtub in the pig pen to water the horses and cattle in, but the main attraction was when the pig got into the tub.

Lorna love her small animals and she loved people, so she never appeared bored as a child. Loren had a hunting dog that had a couple of batches of puppies, and that kept both kids happy.

Lorna liked the puppies best of all. It was not uncommon to find her lying down with the puppies, and the puppies would be all over her and chewing and she would be giggling.

J.B. was amazed with the birthing procedure when he was two years old. We had gone up to see the puppies, and two more were born while we were there. On the way back to the house, J.B. was walking ahead of Lorna and me. He had his little hands crossed behind his back and remarked, "How about that! They came right out of her butt!" Lorna never made any comment.

J.B. explained the procedure to his dad at the supper table. We explained to him that was family talk and not to share it with others, but he did! Laura Withers, the baby sitter, giggled the next day and said, "Guess what J.B. told Holly?" I had no trouble figuring it out. Holly was 18 months old, and Laura and I decided that she was too young for sex education, but J.B. had to tell somebody.

****

When our kids were little, Uncle Bob Eastman bought them a Shetland pony and delivered it to the barn with a big red bow around his neck Yes, it was Christmas time, and when we said "Thanks a lot!" Bob said, "Christmas is the only time of the year a person can get away with that type of delivery!"

The kids loved Uncle Bob for bringing them the pony, just like they loved the pony who they named "Popcorn." We lived next to Highway #31, and the traffic moved at 70 miles an hour, the speed limit, so a Shetland pony could not be trusted to be loose in our yard.

J.B. rode him in the yard, but "Popcorn" was tied to the picnic table. The other place he rode him when we were not by his side was in the corral. Lorna rode the big horse named Dan with close supervision or in the corral. Needless to say, horsemanship was not our kids' best talent. We may have been over-protective, but they lived through childhood in spite of the highway and horses.

****

Loren had three sisters, Mabel Jean Reiser Shively, Nellie Mae Riggin Hall and Dorothy Elizabeth Hallowell

Anderson, with whom he was very close. On my first encounter with Loren's family, I could see how attentive and loving he was with them. I admired his caring ways with his dad, Bryan George Masters, and his mother, Lelia Mae McMurdo Masters.

I believe the old adage, "When a man is good to his mother, he will make a good husband and father!" It held true in our marriage.

Loren's only brother, Jimmy, died shortly after birth before Loren was born, and he always felt cheated. He missed not having a relationship with Jimmy.

Soon after we were married, Tony Young moved to a farm in our neighborhood. He became the brother Loren never had.

Loren had a good pal and a work buddy, and our children were small, and I probably made the most growth spiritually and gained the most emotionally stability during that period of my life. I did not recognize the fact at that time, but it made me strong enough to endure the hardships later on.

We were back in the country, this time on our land, Mortgage Ridge. We owned the place on the hill with Mom and Dad Masters, but now we owned a place of our own and that makes for a big step in life.

We had bought this land when Lorna was a baby and we lived in the outskirts of Topeka. We were unable to move here as the house was not livable, and we had no money for a house of any sort at that time. In fact, we had no money after paying for Lorna's adoption fees and payments on the hill place. The down payment on Mortgage Ridge finished off our saving account.

I was unable to work as a nurse because of the adoption agreement. What to do? I have a wonderful friend who was a manager for Tupperware, Betty Clark. She assured me that the farm payments would be in the bank if I would start selling tupperware under her managing skills. Now all I had to do was convince Loren and find the money for my starter kit.

Like any young family, we wanted security, and that means property of our own! Loren was fairly easy to convince, as he wanted to make all payments on time. Honesty and paying debts on time were very important factors for both Loren and myself.

Now who was to keep Lorna when I held parties? Guess who? Loren Masters. He agreed when I convinced him the profit would be kept for the farm payments. The evening of my first tupperware party made Loren admit he had cold feet about caring for Lorna when she was so little, just a few weeks old.

I pick up my tupperware kit and started for the door as he shook in his boots. I stopped to give him one last hug and a big kiss and patted him on the back and said, "She will be just fine and you cannot learn any younger to care for a small one!" as I smiled and made him blush. After all, he gave excellent care to his patients, and the only difference was the size of the bodies; I had no fear!

My starter kit was paid for with money from the farming account. The profit from my tupperware was banked until the farm payment was due, and the payment was there without fail. It took total dedication from both of us. Thank God, we were willing to do that for our family's future.

Betty Clark is still selling tupperware today, for over forty years. In fact, she still held a party at my house for old-time sake and for her fortieth anniversary in tupperware. She has her own dealership in Hays, Kansas.

Four years had passed after buying Mortgage Ridge before we had living quarters on our farm. Our plans to build a home at that time went down the drain with the rise of inflation. Our nice blueprints were stashed in the bookcase, and we bought a mobile home that we could afford. The mobile home fulfilled our dream on living on Mortgage Ridge.

Now we were living one-half mile from his parents on

the hill place and two miles from Tony Young. Loren and Tony were as different as night and day, but they operated haying equipment and farm machinery as if they had grown up together. Their backgrounds were as different as their personalities, but they molded together in a good working relationship. I wanted to kill both of them at times. They could just aggravate me to tears and they did quite often. But Loren would show up with a "chessy cat " grin on his face and a big wink to make me melt! His big wink melted me down every time.

Before long, Tony would show up with some gift of sorts and all was forgotten. Most of the time Tony's gifts brought me more work in the line of cooking, but his compliments and the pleasing look on his and Loren's faces were worth the anger.

They loved my cooking, and I loved to eat with those old boys! According to today's terminology, we were co-dependent on food. Both of them died to leave me to fight my dependence alone.

After Loren's death, I met lots of people that he worked with over the years at the hospital. Many of them expressed to me how Loren adored me and loved my cooking ability. As I met different ones, they would try to get a recipe that "Masters" had brought to the hospital and they could remember the taste.

Sixteen years later, if Loren and Tony would show up at my table, they would be surprised with my menu! Most of the time I meet friends at the local cafe to avoid lots of left-overs in the refrigerator. Time changes everything and everyone!

When Loren and Tony were alive, I used to serve some "Kansas Beef"! Now my steak, when I have one, is considerably smaller and usually not home-fed unless J.B. feeds one, which makes a tremendous difference.

The only thing Loren and Tony liked better than eating beef was working with cattle and riding their horses. Well, maybe I have reversed those two desires!

Lorna and J.B. were small and I did not know it at that time, but I had everything. I knew I had a good life and later found out it was the best time of my life. One must lose to know what you had! That is a sad fact of life!

****

During the growing years of the children, Loren and I worked at home as well as in nursing. Life was on the run, and the fun was mixed in with the daily routine of life.

After years of living in the mobile home, we had a house moved on Mortgage Ridge. Each move was an improvement in our life, and we would celebrate life with yard parties of one kind or another.

Then the unthinkable happened; Loren was killed while driving the tractor on the highway. J.B. and Bill Riggin were also on the tractor and escaped physical injury.

This event put all of us on a different path for our journey through the rest of our lives. There again, life is a choice, so we got up and dusted off the seat of our pants and went on with life.

****

Several years went by; Bob Eastman developed lung cancer. His treatment plan was long and hard. I took him to radiation, and we had a wonderful time to say good-bye. We reminisced in many ways, talking about old times and how we had fun as children.

I had bought a new pickup, so we traveled all of the back roads to and from radiation. When he could no longer sit up, I drove him in the car where he could lie down in the back seat.

Bob never lost his sense of humor until he lost consciousness, even with all the pain. When he was riding in the back of the car, he said, "Dorf, I never thought I would be rich enough to have my own ambulance!"

On the car tape player, I had all of the old country songs playing that we used to dance to, as we talked of more old memories.

Later when he got so bad, I would lie on the floor besides his bed; he could see if I was awake or asleep. I worked nights and slept at his house after radiation until one of my sisters or his wife came to be with him. One day when I awakened, he was looking down upon me and said, "I never thought I would be rich enough to have a private duty nurse!" With sleep in my eyes I muttered, "Most of them will not sleep on the floor beside you."

Being able to talk through our last days together helped me to work through the loss of my husband, when I did not have a chance to say good-bye.

Being a nurse, I had to deal with death on a regular basis. The ways of working through death are different for everyone. Every death is different. Death is the end result of living; it completes the circle of life.

Knowing that is only part of the game. Living through the death and accepting the end results is quite another.

Watching Bob die by inches helped me to develop my theory of death. During the last few days when Bob was in a very grave condition, I would sit on the porch and look at a big beautiful pink rose bush that was in full bloom with dew.

The dew on the roses made me closer to God as I accepted Bob's death as well as Loren's.

"THE ROSE BUSH THEORY"

I relate life and death to a big, beautiful rose bush. Picture a large blooming rose bush, and you can see your family or a circle of friends. Some of the roses are in full bloom with gorgeous color and perfect shape. Some roses are starting to form buds. Some of the buds never complete the full growing process. Some of the roses are dead and remain on the bush, while others are starting to wither.

Now, relate each and every one of those blooms to different members of your family or your circle of friends, and you can see the life and death process. Life is a process with death being the final phase. Please do not wait, live life to the fullest each and every day.

Keep in mind, to maintain that "rose bush" (loved ones) big and pretty, it must be fed, watered, nurtured, pruned, protected from the elements and loved with gentle caresses and some tender talk. The care is more essential when caring for people.

****

Life is making memories or reliving them. After each death in the family, I would mourn for some time, then start reliving the memories we had made. I feel with my pictures and my memories, I still have everything.

But I feel I have the responsibility to tell my grandchildren the good things about Loren and our life together.

Loren was such a hard-working and fun-loving fellow, but he was more than that. He had a caring heart and would make you feel important.

During our long, slow courtship, I longed for Loren and dreamed how it would be to be Mrs. Loren B. Masters. I had just about given up when it happened.

I had asked Loren to come to a New Year's Eve party after he got off work, but he refused so I went alone. He was working the afternoon shift, and he started thinking about me having fun. After work he got a buddy and started looking for me. Can you believe that? In a town the size of Topeka they started going place to place where he thought I may be.

He never found me as I was at a house party instead of just being out and about. On New Year's Day he called and wanted to go out after work, so we did. He later told me that he had every intention of telling me it was over, but instead he asked me to marry him.

Loren told me his most deepest, darkest secret: he would never have any children. That was not his intention as he planned to break it off without telling me the truth. I loved him with all of my heart, and as well as I loved children, I told him we would work it out.

I cried for days, happy about becoming Loren's wife and very sad because we would never have children. I was living at Carol's house at the time, and I never told her or anyone the truth.

After all, it was Loren's facts, and it was very private. I had no idea what I was doing, but I knew I loved him with all of my heart and whatever will be, will be! Remember it was 1960; people were not as forward with their health facts as today's society. Besides, there was hope!

My birthday is on January the 9th, and Loren was to pick me up after work and take me out to dinner. I had on my prettiest dress and he showed up early. He had asked to get off from work early so he could get to our house before midnight and give me a diamond while it was still my birthday. He popped in the house and gave the ring to me quick.

I was overwhelmed, to say the least! Yes, we had talked about getting married a week earlier, but he had moved so slow during the courtship. I guess he had to do it before he lost his nerve!

I later asked Carol where she was during the excitement and if she knew he was coming with the ring. She just said, "I was out holding up the refrigerator!" but denied knowing about the ring. It is funny how I had on my pretty red dress and Carol knew to get lost at just the right moment! I guess lots of things happen in our head when our heart is at work.

I was working at the Santa Fe Hospital, and the employees were like a family affair. They were as happy for me and very concerned about my happiness. I felt so loved by the attention the co-workers showed and the way they shared my excitement.

We were married on May 21, 1960; my beloved Bob gave me away. We were happy, but our longing for children was always with us. We went to the doctor and had all of the tests done, and it was decided that I would be artificially inseminated.

I became pregnant, and we were so happy until I miscarried. Six months went by as we healed from the miscarriage. No word of adoption had surfaced between us; we were just healing and living life to the fullest.

Out of the blue came the call from Maxine Craig about a baby that needed parents. Loren and I like the idea immediately and started making arrangements.

Lots of things had to be done with a week's notice, but we were on a energy high like none we had ever had before. The arrangements fell into place like clockwork, and we went to pick up our baby girl.

Lorna Mae was the love of our life. The minute she was placed in our arms, she was ours! During the week when we were making arrangements, the lawyer told us the possibility of the natural mother changing her mind during the thirty-day waiting period. We accepted that possibility, but the minute she was in our arms, it was a different story. If necessary, we would fight in court! But thanks be to God, that never happened.

My love for Loren grew as Lorna grew. He was so tender with her; his world was big enough for both of us. Our world wasn't quite complete yet; we needed a baby boy. We did not leave that to chance; we called the Kansas Children's Service League.

J.B. came to live with us when he was ten weeks old. He had been in a foster home while the adoption arrangements were made for us. Here again, as soon as he was placed in our arms, he was ours! Now our family was complete.

****

We worked hard and we played hard. We got lots of living done in our 22 years and had fun along the way. Deep down in our hearts we must have known that our life together had to be fast.

Reflecting back over our life, both of us were driven to accomplish lots in a short time but had fun along the way. We must have known if we were going to do it together — we had to do it now!

****

From the time of Loren's death, my life changed immensely — never to be the same. For years I traveled in high gear, trying to keep up my energy peak up. But age has a way of slowing you down to a dull roar.

What to do with the rest of my life without Loren? I had to find a way to have fun as I slowed down and still keep interested in life.

****

For eleven years I stayed on track, working as a registered nurse and managing the farm. I went at top-notch speed, trying to accomplish everything and to keep Mortgage Ridge looking as if Loren was still helping me. I went on trips periodically to keep up my spirits. All the while getting more fatigued.

The stress was killing me. Having fun turned into a bigger job, and the job turned into a nightmare. Something had to give!

One night as I was running down the hall for supplies to care for a patient, I heard a voice that stopped me in my tracks. It was Loren's voice, "Get the Hell out of here!" I turned around and the hall was empty, and the voice continued, "We've worked too hard, for you —." Then there was dead silence in the hall.

As soon as my patient was stable, I started thinking about what I had heard. I knew it was a sign and I had to act. I wrote out a resignation and gave two weeks' notice.

My boss was astounded, as were all of my coworkers. But I was serious, and two weeks later I walked away from hospital nursing and full-time employment at the age of 57.

My belief is, life is a choice and I chose life. Life in the fast lane was killing me, and I had to find a way to survive and slow down. After all, Mortgage Ridge is a haven and that's where I wanted to be.

Loren and I planned to be together on Mortgage Ridge for our final years, but all I have is his memory. As I sit here this morning and listen to the birds sing and watch the flag fly in the breeze, I feel his presence.

That night when I heard his voice, I later thought "what to do?" Write about my experiences. First, I had to learn how to write. I bought a word processor and started taking writing workshops. Then I needed exposure, so I started writing for the local newspapers to improve my skill at writing.

Over five years passed before starting this book. I had worn out my word processor, so I bought a computer.

****

The death of my sweet Loren has made me appreciate life so such more fully. I never knew what I had when I had it! One truly has to lose to learn to appreciate. What a sad fact of life!

My memories keep me going on in life. Each day I reach out for fun and laughter. I drive through the Flint Hills of Kansas and admire the beauty around me. When I was young and riding my horse in the Flint Hills, I didn't appreciate the beauty.

The big fluffy clouds have always been overhead. The wild flowers have always been in bloom during the season. But now I appreciate each and everything around me. The butterflies have always flown, but now I watch in total amazement.

****

Loren had some bad habits as well as good points. One of his bad points was the fact he laughed when people fell down. His mother was kind of clumsy, and she would fall down just any place and he would laugh. I would get angry at him for laughing, and his mother would laugh with him.

I told him that if I ever fell and he laughed, I would beat the Hell out of him. One day we were waxing Bessie's car in the garage and I slipped down. I noticed that Loren disappeared. Sure enough, he had gone behind the garage to laugh. I sneaked upon him and he was laughing, so I

158

beat on him until he begged for mercy. But he was still laughing; he said, "But you looked so funny!"

****

Loren liked me to work outside with him and I preferred outside work, but the indoor work had to be done sometime. He would beg me to just go with him and I would not have to do a thing. Boy, did I get tired doing "nothing"! Ha, that would have been the day!

But on the other hand, he was real good about helping me to do the inside work in a hurry so I could help him out of doors.

One time my cousin, Doris Steege, was visiting the Santa Fe Trails Nursing Home in Burlingame while I was working. She said, "I did not expect you to be at work today!" When I asked why, she said, "There's a wash hanging on the clothesline."

I told her Loren was off today and he probably did the wash. She exclaimed, "But there were white clothes on the line!" I told her, "Loren knows how to do white clothes also."

****

When it was Loren's day off from the hospital, he had things he was planning to do regardless of the weather. I was always trying to get him to wait until the weather was just right. He would win out and we would attempt to accomplish the task.

Loren's mom wanted to watch the children so I would be out with him, to keep him from doing the impossible, but that didn't always work!

She had a good reason for wanting someone out with him. Dad and Loren were working on the combine in the yard one day and a spring broke and knocked Dad out. Loren had to hold the combine off Dad and was unable to pull him out from underneath at the same time. Loren yelled and Mom heard him and came outside and pulled Dad out from beneath the combine. That convinced her they needed help at all times when working outside of the yard.

159

She would beg me to leave the children with her and help Loren. She was afraid of Loren getting hurt and no one there to help him. She should have been more afraid that he would hurt me in process!

One day I left the kids with her and went with Loren to fell a tree across the creek and change the flow of the creek. It sounded simple. The only trouble, the wind was blowing from the wrong direction.

Loren had me on the south side of the creek on the tractor. He had the tractor hooked to the tree with a cable across the creek. The tractor was sitting on frosty ground (bad for traction).

Loren got up in the tree with his chain saw. I said, "Loren, when you saw that tree loose, the wind is going to blow the tree to the north and pull me and the tractor into the creek where you wanted the tree. He disagreed. I quit him and walked to the house. His mother said, "Where is Loren?" I told her that he was being unreasonable and I came home to live with the kids.

He quit the job and came to the house. The next time he did it when I was at work. I guess the wind changed, as he lived and accomplished the job.

But let me say on his behalf, Loren was not doing anything dangerous when he was killed, as farmers have to be on the highway to get from field to field and to do their feeding chores. He was killed on the highway on a hill by a car/tractor accident. Accidents happen!

Farming is dangerous at times, and working with machinery can be accident-prone. A car can become a lethal weapon when conditions are just right.

****

Before we had children, Mom would work outside with us and so would Dad when he was feeling good.

One day Loren decided to burn a large hedge pile, so we set it afire and watched it burn. The middle burnt out, leaving the edges not burning well. Loren thought he would cable the tractors together and he would drive one and I would drive the other tractor and pull in the burning hedge.

Things were going good, and then Loren on the bigger tractor started pulling me into the fire. The middle of the fire starting burning good after being stirred. I couldn't get Loren's attention as he pulled me into the fire. I jumped off the tractor and ran where he could see me and pointed, "It is your tractor, you go get it!" And he did.

He could be dangerous, as he was so determined to get his work done on his day off! Later, he would laugh about it, but not when there was work to be done.

****

Loren loved big hedge posts, and he could build a real fence with just the right hedge for fence posts. He would cut the hedge and trim out the posts for the fence he was making. One day he came to the house to get me to help him move the corner post and the brace post he had cut.

There was one problem. He had not cut the brace post off the corner post. I quickly said, "Cut the brace post off so we can lift it."

He said, "I do not know just where I want to cut it yet!" He added, "Let's take it up to the pasture where I can measure them."

I said, "It is too heavy for me to lift my share."

He said, "You could lift it you wanted to!"

He made me so mad that I grabbed hold of it and we put it in the truck. I was strong as a horse then, and when I got mad something had to give!

Well, when we got it in the truck, it was too long and too heavy for the truck. I proceeded to get up into the truck and sit on the trunk to hold it in the pickup so Loren could drive it to its destination.

Everything went fine until we drove across the creek. The brace end caught and started pulling the post and me out of the truck.

I yelled to stop. Loren stopped and I got out and pushed

it back into the truck and held it until he crossed the creek. Then I had to get back in and sit on it until we reached the place in the pasture where it was to be set.

The next day Glenn Taylor and Tony Young asked him how he got that post up to the pasture. Loren said, "I made Dorothy mad enough she lifted it!"

It took three good men to set the post after he had cut off the brace portion. Loren heard about that post more than once, but he took his ribbing from the guys who were out hunting for years to come.

The first pasture season after Loren's death when the pasture was burned, so was that fence post. How ironic!

****

My brother, Jack, was just buried June 19, 1998, and when I was out in Colorado for his burial, many memories came to mind.

Jack had a unique sense of humor, and with Loren's shenanigans they were quite a pair. Loren like to collect antiques; one time when we were in Colorado and out for a ride on Gold Camp Road, Loren saw an old railroad spike. Jack stopped so Loren could pick it up for his collection.

Before we got down out of the mountains, both Jack and Loren had quite a story about the spike and the railroads in the mountains. Jack wanted me to write the story that went with the spike. I did not, the story was pure bull!

I remember well how much fun we used to have when both Jack and Loren were alive and our trips to Colorado and their trips back home. Sitting around the kitchen table and cracking jokes, and could Jack tell jokes, not all of them clean.

One time when we were out there, Jack was driving and a lady was coming up the mountain pass the wrong way, so Jack told her. She kept right on going and said, "I know, I know!" J.B. would repeat her each and every time; it fit for the rest of the trip. He decided to get into the act of cutting up like Loren and Jack. I can close my eyes and hear them cutting up and laughing and having fun. Their laughter was contagious.

Most of our family had a good sense of humor; therefore, our laughs were frequent when they were alive, but all of them are dead now except Liz and I.

But the memories linger on in my mind, and I laugh without them, just thinking about what they used to say and do.

****

Before we had children, Loren and I rented a camper for the back of the pick-up and took my mother with us to visit Bessie in St. Louis.

We had been advised by Uncle Doug McMurdo "to rent one of the damn things!" before buying a camper. Before our trip was over we understood why he wanted us to rent.

First of all, it leaked and our bed was wet for the first night. We hung out our bedding the next day while at Bessie's, just as if they was a bed wetter among us..

We did not have big mirrors and had a terrible time seeing where we were going on the six-lane bypass in St. Louis.

After visiting Bessie, we fished in Missouri, and everything was just fine until I started to fix supper. Nothing would stay on the stove because we did not have leveling jacks for the camper. Mother sat with potholders and held the pots on the stove as I cooked our supper.

Needless to say, we did not want to buy or rent another camper when we got home. That did it for us and our camping; motels are the way to go.

****

One more thing about brother Jack, he had a habit of saying after a joke, "Write it down, it is a good one!" But he did not live to see this book in print. Another sad fact of life.

****

The last year of Loren's life we worked together again at the V.A. Hospital, so we rode together and would go directly to Lorna and J.B.'s ball games. Loren would be driving me and I would sit in the back seat with a cooler of sandwich meat, making sandwiches for the ball teams to eat on the bus during their ride home. J.B. was usually slow getting to the bus and the sandwiches were gone, so he would have to wait until he got in the car at Mission Valley.

Loren would get cute and look in the rear view mirror and say, "Mrs._____ could make sandwiches, but she works!"

He would have to rub in. I was delegated to call mothers of the team players and ask them to donate sandwiches. If I met with any resistance like working moms or any other excuses, I just made the sandwiches instead of begging someone to do it.

Lorna helped with two teams and J.B. played on two teams, so sometimes we would be on the bleachers almost as many hours as we were at work that day.

But it was all worth it to see the kids involved in sports and enjoying themselves. After Loren's death I had to enjoy all of the activities twice as much for both of us.

Loren only got to watch J.B. play football one year, when he was a freshman. The next three years I thought about the song, "Blind Man in the Bleachers" by Kenny Starr, as I watched J.B. run with the ball. In the song the blind man died, so his son knew he could then see him run the ball.

Lorna was almost ready to graduate when her father was killed, and what a hard time it was for her. Not to have her daddy see her graduate.

****

Loren was always neat and found a place for everything in the garage and also in the house when he was asked to store things away. He had hung an electric heater from the ceiling of the basement. Many years after his death I got the heater down for someone to use.

I noticed something red pushed over the ceiling of J.B.'s room in the basement. Being curious as to what that red thing was, I pulled it out. Much to my surprise, it was a red-handled pool cue. No one agreed to having stashed it above the ceiling.

I hardly think Loren stashed it there. To this day, that pool cue stands in my basement without an owner, and no one, but no one, has admitted to being its owner. Do you find that strange?

****

Everybody comments about my fast pace! Well, I have to take two quick short steps to everyone's normal stride. My legs are short and I learned at a young age to walk fast to keep up. My dad was a tall, brawny man for the times. He would not be considered tall today, but he seemed tall in the forties.

One time we were going out across the pasture and he tapped me on the back of the legs. I was so surprised I turned and said, "Why did you do that?"

He answered, "You are walking too slow!" I thought about that as I hastened my step. I never forgot that ,and I walk like I'm really going some place everywhere I go.

Over the years I have tried to figure out that day. I have finally decided I started out ahead of Dad and was poking along when he caught up with me and tapped me.

Nonetheless, I take no chances today. I walk fast everywhere I am going.

****

Sex education: One evening I was sitting on the corral gate and the bull started jumping up on a cow. I started yelling, "Dad, he is going to kill that cow!"

Dad was in the corral talking to some guy about selling cattle. Bob knocked me off the gate. I got up and dusted off myself and ask, "Why did you do that?"

Bob replied, "To get your mind on other things." Bob was three and a half years older, and I supposed some of the older kids gave him the same type of treatment when he became curious about sex.

165

My mother gave me a box of Kotex and said, "You'll be needing these once a month!" Those were the days of few instructions. Learn the best way you can, alley education or whatever! Oh, she also told me, "Don't mess with boys!"

Times had really changed by the time our children were growing up. I had told my mother, "I am going to raise my kids differently as I do not want them to grow up as dumb as I grew up."

Before I could start sex education with Lorna, she floored me. I was washing a turkey in the sink and had my hand in the cavity washing out the inside and Lorna asked, "Are you getting the baby out?"

I was utterly amazed! She was approximately two years old and was standing beside me on a step stool to see the sink. I guess she had seen the birthing procedure on television before she was two.

One day we were riding in the truck and J.B. was standing behind his dad. Mother Eastman, Lorna and I were also in the truck, and as we drove out across the pasture, J.B. pointed out one of the cows to Loren and said, "Dad, I saw the bull bred that cow yesterday."

Mother took a long breath and heaved a sigh. I know she thought to herself, "What is this world coming to?"

****

Bob Eastman had a theory about Social Security, and I heard him say it many times, "By God, they ought to give you your Social Security when you are young enough to enjoy it because every old fart wants to work anyway!" But he never lived to get his Social Security as he died when he was 54 years old. His theory may have worked for him.

As for the Golden Years, they not very golden for some people, as it seems to be the time for repairs and maintenance after one gets older.

It sure is nice to sit back and draw the easy money after retirement. But fun on the run is slowed down considerably!

****

Loren served for the United States Army during the Korean War and was stationed at the Panama Canal. He had lots of pictures from his days in that area and confessed he had the good life as he drove the jeep for the base commander.

He told me about it after the fact and said many times, "I wish you had been my girl while in the Panama, as you would have written lots of love letters to pass the time. He said he ate lots of bananas waiting for time to pass while at the canal. He also confessed to drinking his share of rum and coke.

The Panama Canal is a waterway that cuts across the Isthmus of Panama which links the Atlantic Ocean with the Pacific Ocean. This allows ships to cut through the canal to shorten the trip from New York to San Francisco instead of having to go down around the bottom of the South American continent.

The locks amazed Loren as to how they locked in the water to raise the ships up so they could pass through the canal to the other ocean.

The United States built the Panama Canal at a cost of around $380 million during a ten-year span in the early 1900s. Loren was sent there to defend the canal, as were other soldiers for many years.

All of his effort to defend the canal was lost in 1971 as the United States when new negotiations were started for a new treaty. The Panama Canal Commission will take over the control of the canal on December 31, 1999.

****

When I started going places with Loren, he had such a baby face and an adorable smile. He did not look his age for sure, which was 26 years old at the time. If he wanted to buy liquor, he had to show identification which made him feel inferior. I always looked older than my age, and I told him it would make me feel good if they ever asked for my identification.

Loren grew hair on his chest after we were married, and

I would smile at him and say, "I made a man out of you!"

If I would call him a "boy," he would quickly say, "How big do men grow where you came from?" He was rough and ready, but under that gruff exterior was a real pussy cat, but he did not want many folk to know. When I would tell him what a big pussy cat he was, he would wink and grab me.

****

My dad had a theory about cleaning house. My mother always cleaned our house from top to bottom when she was going to have club. Dad thought that was foolish and would say, "Wait until after the party to clean, when it ready needs it!"

He had a good point, why clean before and after?

Loren had a theory when I would be doing some extra cleaning for company; he would remark, "If it is good enough for us all the time, it will be good enough for company for a couple of hours!"

They both had a good point, and over the years I have developed a plan for cleaning my house. I do what I want and when I want to do it. Which means I keep it clean enough for me and hopeful everyone else can stand the place while they are here!

****

My dad was a real "mule skinner" in his day. Working with mules was a real art, and as he said many times, "First, you have to get their attention!" That theory today would be challenged by many animal activists!

In the thirties he worked for the W.P.A. when the Wabaunsee Lake was built. He rode one of his mules over every day (about four or five miles across the pastures), taking his lunch and feed for the mules. With his mules and the slip, he moved dirt and helped to build the dam. His pay was $1 per day! That was in the early thirties when work was hard and everything was done the hard way and salaries were very cheap.

A dollar a day doesn't seem like much, but it helped him

168

feed his family and stay alive after the Great Depression.

He also built quite a reputation with his mules, as La Moyne Mercer recently stated in the local newspaper that Fred Eastman could have built the bridge on Highway #31 with his mules in two months, and it had taken the construction company over seven months.

I loved her comparison even if it was stretching the truth.

Dad was also a horse trader, and he would buy anything that he thought he could make some money. I remember some old pigs that were nearly starved to death before he brought them. My mother had a fit when she saw the pigs as she knew he borrowed money to buy them. But he made a few dollars on the pigs.

Then there was the time he brought home an extra skinny horse that had been neglected. The horse turned out to be one of our better riding horses after Dad fed him and got him in shape for riding. My dad would buy or trade anything he had; in fact, he threatened to trade me off a time or two.

****

There was a C.C.C. Camp at Lake Wabaunsee, and during World War II German Prisoners were housed in the old barracks. They worked for farmers in the area; Dad hired them during harvest. Mother, Helen and I would take them a mid-meal snack to the field, as well as water throughout the day, besides cooking a noon meal for them.

As a child, I remember very little about the experience, but I recall how different it seemed that they were unable to speak English.

There was a guard with them, and he had a gun which stood out in my mind. It was very unusual for a gun to be in our daily routine.

Bob was bitten by a German Police Dog during their time at the farm. Bob with his sense of humor swore, "That damn dog was supposed to bite the Germans!"

****

When Loren and I were first married, lagoons systems

were fairly new and we did not know anything about them. During our walking exercise in the area of our home on the Quail Place, we found what we thought was a small pond in the surrounding mile from the house. There were wild ducks on the "pond."

We thought, "Wait until duck hunting season and we will go."

Time went by and duck season came; Loren took the gun and we went for our walk. When we got close to the "pond," we laid down and crawled up the bank, Army style, so as not to scare off the ducks.

Sure enough, there were ducks and Loren shot one. When we walked to the other side of the "pond" to pick up the duck, it was floating in a bunch of turds.

"Now we know why there are dams on all four sides!" This must be a lagoon system!

Well, we took the duck home and cleaned it, and the next day was my day off, so I cooked it. I decided to bake it in wine to take away the wild taste. During the afternoon the smell of that duck cooking in wine with its unusual smell, when I closed my eyes, I could see those turds floating on the water.

By supper time, I told Loren he could eat the duck if he wanted, but I had decided I did not want duck. Loren could not smell and it made no difference to him; it just made more for him and did he enjoy meat of any kind.

Years later, when we told that story to the Haag's, George gave me a no-fail recipe for baking wild duck. But no more wild-duck cooking for me, as that smell lingered on in my mind for years.

But I must share George Haag's recipe for baking a wild duck. "Put the wild duck on a shake shingle and bake it at 400 degrees for four hours. Throw away the duck and eat the shingle!"

I knew he was joking when he got to the amount of degrees and baking time, but it let me know what he thought of wild ducks.

****

When I was nursing school, I was asked to give readings for programs for the doctors on occasions. One time I gave the following poem:

> At sweet sixteen, I first began,
> To ask dear, Santa, for a man.
> At seventeen, you will recall,
> I wanted someone strong and tall.
> The Christmas when I reached eighteen,
> I wanted someone dark and lean.
> And at nineteen, I was sure
> I'd fall for someone more mature.
> At twenty, I still thought I'd find
> Romance in someone with a mind.
> I retrogressed at twenty-one
> And found the college boys more fun.
> My viewpoint changed at twenty-two,
> I longed for someone to be true.
> He broke my heart, at twenty-three,
> I begged for someone to be kind to me.
> Then, asked at last at twenty-four,
> Anyone who wouldn't bore.
> Santa, now that I am twenty-five,
> Just send me someone who's alive!!!!

So much for the Christmas party for the doctors when I was a student. I got those jobs because I liked to show off a bit now and then. It is amazing that the nuns encouraged us to be funny!

Forty years passed and I had forgotten the poem and the Christmas party that the students gave to the doctors. The doctors gave the students many pounds of Russell Stover Candy each Christmas, so the nuns had the students give them a party.

Vicky Ramirez Webb sent me an aged copy of the poem

in her Christmas letter in 1997, and it brought back many good memories. It reminded me of another time the nuns gave me the day off to rest my voice so I would be able to give a reading at the doctors' party. That reading was about dieting, and I wish I had a copy of that reading to share with you.

The Christmas poem was not true in the end, as I snagged Loren when I was twenty-four, and he met all of the requirements and then some. He certainly never bored me.

****

One night at the supper table, I said to Loren, "I've overdone it!" He looked at me so strange and said, "What are you talking about?"

I asked him "if he remembered when we were first married and I asked him if he wanted me save money by having a light supper occasionally to save money on the grocery bill?"

His reply, "I'll work good every day if you will fix me a good supper every evening!"

Loren had forgotten the conversation until I reminded him, and he was unable to make the connection until I told him we had two freezers and they were bulging at the seams and he and I were bulging at the seams. Then it made sense!

Loren died a happy man, as he loved to eat and I loved to cook for him.

****

Now that I think about it, Loren would have been happier if I had continued to cook him eggs every morning for breakfast as I once did. Medical research had started talking about cholesterol, and the egg scare had me back off daily eggs.

As it turned out, I wished I had fixed all of the eggs he wanted, but at the time I felt I was doing the right thing.

****

Bob Eastman ate just what he liked and dared anyone to try to change his diet, even for health reasons. If one would try to get Bob to eat something because it was healthy for him, he would remark, "Even Euell Gibbons died!"

For those of you that do not remember Euell Gibbons, he was big on nature and professed to eat lots of wild berries and nuts and highly nutritional foods that seemed strange to most people during his lifetime.

What a difference a few decades makes in the theories of diet as well as everything!

****

Loren loved antiques. He liked the ones that were handed down in the family, especially the old tools and such. He was quite a collector of junk, or at least that is what I called it.

Loren would get old tools, horse collars and parts of harness from different relatives. He would paint them up and display them in our "Hut."

The "Hut" was a room that we built on the east side of our garage for storage and for entertaining company when we lived in our trailer house.

Some old antiques he painted and displayed in the yard as yard art. He liked my dad's one-horse corn planter. It sat on our well curb until it rusted into pieces.

****

When I was a new graduate nurse at the V.A. Hospital, I wanted to collect a urine sample from one of the mental patients.

I asked the patient to urinate into this bottle and he ignored me. One of the seasoned aides said, "Let me collect it for you!" So I handed him the container.

He took the patient into the latrine, and I followed to the door to hear his technique.

The aide said, "Piss in this bottle!" The patient said, "Ah, go shit in the creek!" as he walked away.

The aide came out and handed me the bottle. I smiled and said, "Your language didn't help a bit, as we still do not have a specimen."

****

I am deathly afraid of snakes, and I taught both Loren and his dad not to tease me about snakes.

The first time Loren and I went to Gage Park Zoo, we were in the snake building, which was dark. All of the snakes were in glassed cages; I was standing looking at the snakes when Loren poked me in the ribs.

When I came to my senses, I was beating Loren on top of his head with my purse and he was grinning from ear to ear.

I told him later he made me make a fool of myself, but he never again played a trick on me when it came to snakes.

Loren's dad, Bryan, learned the same lesson the hard way. We were getting a drill out of an old building, and the grass was real tall where I could not see where I was walking.

Dad ran out of the shed and yelled, "Snake!" I ran out on high and when I got out there, Dad laughed; there was no snake.

Without thinking, I grabbed Dad by the shoulders and shook him like a rat, saying, "Don't you ever do that again, ole man!"

When I came to my senses, I thought maybe Loren would grab me, but he never, as he knew the old man had it coming when he surprised me with that joke.

In time of surprise I acted and then thought about it, and Loren knew that well. There were no more snakes jokes. Loren told me later, "Dad is just as scared as you are when it comes to snakes!"

****

I have always been very independent. Even in childhood I was determined to do things for myself. When I was sixteen, I went to Dr. Pratt's office to get a tooth pulled and went back downtown to pick up my Mother and the groceries with ten teeth missing instead of the one I had gone to get pulled.

Mother had a fit. Her first words were, "How will we

ever pay for your dentures?" I told her, "I have that worked out with Dr. Pratt!"

After all, it was my mouth and most parents did not have to buy their children dentures. I had a terrible Christmas. When you are young and unable to eat candy because of a toothache, it is the end of the world, especially at Christmas time.

I had discussed with the dentist about pulling my teeth, a few at a time, during the last semester of school and going without them for the summer and he would have my teeth ready and I would be adjusted to them before the next school year. So he pulled ten instead of just one.

I had arranged with him to pay him the following summer when I could get a job, and he agreed. No questions were asked of my parents. The plans were made by the dentist and myself. That could not be done today because of liability. No dentist would trust you for payment for over a year. No one would push their liability insurance that far today. Besides, I was a minor child!

I lived in Topeka with Bessie the next summer and got a job. I was doing waitress work at the Purple Cow, which was the coffee shop in the Hotel Kansan at 10th and Kansas Avenue.

I worked afternoons and walked home after eleven, which was about ten blocks. It would not be safe today to walk downtown in the dark or anywhere else. But I paid for my dentures, sheer determination.

The next summer after we graduated high school, Carol Weekes Swenson stayed with Bessie and me, and we worked at the Purple Cow. What a time we had!

We worked during the day shift and walked both ways. Up and down Kansas Avenue, we had plenty of laughs along the way, believe me.

Bessie would not let both of us sleep with her except when the weather was too bad for us to sleep on the glassed-in porch. As Carol said, "We had lots of bad nights on the porch!"

175

During that summer I made enough to pay for my first year of college. That couldn't be done now either. Of course, times were different, to say the least. Very little money was spent on recreation, and that was a good thing because there was no money for recreation. A typical Saturday night for Carol and me was buying a watermelon for a treat.

****

Brother Jack more or less encouraged me to write a book, as this was his favorite saying when someone told a good joke: "Write that down, it is a good one!" Writing this book helps me to remember Jack and all of the our laughs together.

It has been a great source of healing!

****

When my family was not making me laugh, my patients did, and they keep me laughing for several decades. Many of them could say the cutest things and be so innocent.

Once I had a patient who was dying of cancer and I went in the check his I.V., and he called me an old fruit jar which tickled me. I laughed and walked out of the room thinking he said that because of my being short and squatty.

Days later I read his obituary and found out his was a collector and dealer in antique fruit jars. So I guess that was a rare compliment.

Another time comes to mind: a lady was sitting in a big chair between the beds of a nursing home where I was working. I was making her bed and she reached out and swatted by behind.

I said, "You better watch that!"

She smiled cutely and said, "Why, will it go off?"

Those are the kind of things that made my day! Their cute remarks made all of the aches and pains of working hard on a dead run worth my time and energy.

Working in a nursing home setting for 15 years brought lots of smiles to my face, as no one is as dear as a little old innocent person. Besides, working in a nursing close to home allowed me to attend school events with Lorna and J.B.

One man in the nursing home comes to mind with the present-day problem with sexual encounters of President William Clinton, or "Slick Willy" as he is called. His name was Chet and he chased all of the girls in the nursing home, and once in awhile he caught one!

The nursing staff were constantly after Chet to keep him away him from the female patients that couldn't ran so fast. I tried, as Director of the Nursing, to solve Chet's problem.

First of all, I checked with the physician to see if "Salt Peter" was a possibility for a cure. I guess I should have been seeking it for the White House! Only it doesn't work except psychologically!

The doctor laughed when I asked. So I tried another angle. I took Chet down to his wife's house for the afternoon.

The wife took all precautions; she had one of her neighbors there when we arrived, and another one was there when I picked Chet up.

We continued to chase him away from the ladies, but he was quick and would slip his hand up under a dress in a flash. This continued until his death, so I guess the country and "Slick Willy" will just carry on!

After all, the saying, "You can't break an old dog from eating eggs or chasing cars," must be true!

On a different note, my mother was teasing me about getting home after a date when I was in college and home for the weekend. I told her, "We had a flat tire!"

She smiled and said, "Dorothy, can't you come up with some excuse better than that?"

I remarked, "Well, it is the truth!"

She continued to smile as if she didn't believe me. So I decided to tease her. I said, "Now just what excuse did you use?"

She grinned and said, "Well, we had to rest the horses, didn't we?"

It just proves, sex never changes, just new players every few years, and some people play harder than others and some play for keeps.

****

I remember my dad telling my brothers, "Boys, when you reach forty, you'll be a real man!" I assumed it worked the same for girls! When I reached forty years of age, I expected to become a real woman!

Well, I lost faith in my daddy's words of wisdom! I did not grow any more in physical strength after forty, but I matured with wisdom. Or at least I like to think that I have! Dad may have being saying that.

****

But my life with Loren was not all rosy! There were bad times but, thank God, there were more good times than bad. Many times I wanted to kill him for a few minutes. I have a bad temper and, of course, it was worse when I were younger.

I could get mad in a minute, blow my "stack," mouth off good and then get over it. When Loren got mad, he was mad for days. After it was all over and we were laughing and making up, I would tell him, "If you would just snub me down and kiss me, it would be all over!"

He would reply, "Would I kiss a rattlesnake?"

The making up was worth all of the bad times. Each and every fuss made me love him more.

One time comes to mind when I did not get over my mad spell right away. We were over in the Gifford pasture sorting cattle. Loren thought I could do everything! When he wanted a critter caught, he wanted it done regardless. That is at the moment; later he would laugh at how ridiculous he really was.

This particular time at the Gifford place, an 800-lb. critter would not turn into the spot Loren wanted her to go, and when I saw it was me or the critter, I stepped aside. Loren yelled, "By God, you could have stopped her if you wanted to!"

It made me so mad and I stayed mad for a couple of days. In fact, I refused to dance with him that night! I loved to dance but not that night. J.B. still teases me about the episode.

****

As I mentioned earlier, Loren and I again worked together at the V.A. Hospital before his death. Not many days before his death, while at work, I ran into him over at the canteen.

I was surprised to see him, and he winked with that look in his eye. Just like that old days, the thrill was still there.

I can close my eyes and see his wink today.

Part III

LIFE IS A CHOICE

PREFACE

I wanted to share my feelings and thoughts about my personal and professional experiences with others. I had the opportunity to have a good life, thanks to God, my family, my friends and last but not least, my patients.

I was blessed in my nursing career to have worked with many kind people with outstanding knowledge, most of whom were willing to share their knowledge with me. In return, I wanted to share with you.

The nursing profession is a demanding career, but the rewards are many. Like any profession, there are all kinds of people and that makes for a well-rounded life with untold experiences.

I am sure that each and everyone has a different story to tell at the end of their professional career because people develop unique attitudes about living and dying. This must be different for everyone as we all have an individual sense of values and different emotional outlets. I feel that everyone is a product of his background, life experiences, educational opportunities and intellectual abilities.

I hope this book will be a benefit to you in living the rest of your life as it has been a rewarding experience for me to be able to share.

One of my impressions for writing the book would have been 100 years old today, November 27, 1995. My dad, Fred Eastman, was born on this day in 1895. He died of lung cancer when I was 19 years old and a junior in nursing.

Another impression for writing this book was the life and death of my late husband, Loren B. Masters, whom I will always love and admire. Loren, like my parents taught me many things about life in general.

In 1999, I got the courage to rewrite this book and have it printed.

DEDICATION

To my children and beloved late husband,
You made my life and choices worthwhile.

To my family and friends,
Thanks for the extra love and attention.

To the people involved in my career,
Thanks for the extended love.

Thanks, God, for making it all possible.

THANKS

I wish to thank Teresa Oliver of Burlingame, Kansas, for her help in editing and her encouragement for me to trudge on with my endeavor. Teresa, I shall never forget your kindness to me and your help with my writing career.

18

As I RAN down the hospital corridor, I heard a familiar voice, "Get the Hell out of here!" I glanced over my left shoulder, but no one was there. I continued my trip down the hall for supplies and the voice sounded again, "We have worked too hard for —" and the voice drifted away.

Since I was giving critical care to an elderly gent, I continued my journey with many questions on my mind.

I was very troubled with many aspects of nursing and life running rampant through my mind while stabilizing the patient's condition. My mind was full of changes in nursing and medical approaches that I had witnessed during my career.

I was nursing an old gent with terminal cancer, our medical team was putting more tubes in his body and the patient was pulling out the tubes. To me, he was saying, leave me alone — and let me die in peace! When you are a part of a medical team, you do as the majority of the team decides whether you fully agree or not..

Making people suffer with heroic measures was the change in medical and nursing practices that bothered me the most. We, the medical community, do not always honor the patient's wishes pertaining to living wills. Quality of life is so important to me as an individual; therefore, just sustaining quantity of life became very difficult for me as the assisting nurse.

My joints, in fact, my whole body was squealing, "I cannot take this dead run approach of hospital nursing until the calendar says that my retirement is in the mail!" My body and mind had been going full-tilt for thirty-nine years with nursing details, plus a very active private life. So why was I surprised with my body complaining?

For various reasons, I had not stayed in the same position for all of those years. So I could not just retire. At age fifty-seven, I needed and wanted to work until retirement age, both for financial security as well as for a completed accomplishment. When you add thirty-nine and eight years, the sum sounds unbelievable for a person's endurance of running halls and stooping over beds. Eight years until I would be sixty-five, seemed like an eternity!

When I had time to take a deep breath after stabilizing the patient, I tried to figure out the voice that had stopped me in my tracks earlier. I knew that familiar voice was that of Loren B. Masters, my late husband. He and I had worked in that veteran's hospital many years ago. But Loren had been dead for eleven years! Loren and I had been married for twenty-two years before he was killed. When he used that tone of voice, someone was in great danger!

I then realized that he, as my Guardian Angel, was telling me to quit work and enjoy myself on our country property while I still had time.

As a nurse and a mother, I had said many times, "Life is a CHOICE," when explaining options to my patients or my children about their health. Now it was my time to make a big choice! Do I continue to work and risk my health further or do I quit and change my spending habits? I chose to quit!.

Later that night, when time permitted, I wrote out a resignation giving two weeks' notice. I shocked everyone who knew me, including myself.

I personally handed the resignation to my head nurse at quitting time. She was mighty surprised and replied, "Well, you can't quit because you will not get any money for several years!" I responded quickly, "Oh, yes, I can. I own three hundred and twenty acres, and if I haven't saved any money in thirty-nine years, I deserve to graze with the cattle!"

The head nurse did not like to take "no" for an answer, so she added, "Hold on until we can get you some help!" I answered, "This place is killing me, and I will be leaving two weeks from right now! Money is no good to you when you are dead!"

A big weight lifted from my shoulders immediately. I was able to work with a big smile on my face once again. I knew my sense of humor had dwindled, but until I heard Loren's warning voice, I did not realize that my humor had vanished completely.

Two weeks later as I carried out my fifteen roses, one for each year, the head nurse said, "Come back in thirty days and nothing will change." She was talking about policy, salary and benefits, and I stated, "I know that and I won't be back, but thanks anyway!" I knew that staffing and other problems would also not change, and I had taken all I could endure without my sense of humor.

I had been working the night shift exclusively for the last nine years to avoid having to work a rotation of all three shifts. As a floor duty nurse in a federal hospital, I had worked all three shifts and more than my share of holidays and weekends. So the night shift seemed like a breeze for a few years with set nights off to let my body and mind get accustomed to resting on a regular basis.

Lots of my friends thought the night shift was my biggest problem, and I am sure that was part of the problem. Working the night shift is against the rules of nature as we are supposed to sleep every night, not just every fifth and sixth night! But me and my aging body chose not to go back to the day shift and rotate through all three shifts.

Finally my Guardian Angel, Loren, set me free! I thank him and God for the guidance. I am very glad that I heeded the warning! Loren knew I was not any good to myself, my family or my patients without my sense of humor to carry us through. I have never been sorry that I followed his suggestion.

My stomach churned several times between the time of turning in my resignation and my final night's work, wondering if I had made the right decision. It is hard to walk away from a $40,000+ per year job as if one does not need money to exist. Usually fear keeps people in a job past their productive years. Many people have big debts forcing them to stay in a position. There again, life is a choice, and I chose to manage my money without large debts. One co-worker said, "You can't quit, you won't get any retirement pay for several years!" I replied, "Yes, I can, as I do not have a boat payment!"

My daughter-in-law, Jean, never knew the real me until I resigned. She had been in the family only a few years, but my sense of humor had been slowly dwindling because of stress and exhaustion. A few days after I wrote out my resignation, Jean stated, "You act as though a big weight has been lifted from your head!" I replied, "Yes, just making the decision to quit working so hard in such a stressful environment helped me find my humor again!"

A couple weeks prior to resigning, I had interviewed for a different type of nursing position. My daughter, Lorna Mae, was aware of the interview, but she was shocked when she heard that I had resigned. Lorna spoke to me after the family dinner where she had heard the shocking news, "Mom, I thought that you were going to change jobs. I did not know that you had quit!" I answered, "I just quit today and have two weeks to work!" She looked puzzled but said no more.

After resigning, I did not see Lorna until dinnertime at a family dinner where I mentioned my resignation to my brother-in-law as we went through the buffet line. The news traveled around the restaurant mighty quick. My sisters-in-laws really cheered when they heard the news, and one of them remarked, " I was afraid you were going to let that job kill you!"

Earlier,when I told my son, J.B., that I was going to change jobs sometime, he said, "Mom, I would hate to see you quit your job!" I looked him in the eye and said, "Son, you have no idea what I have to do every night!" He had a serious, puzzled look but remained speechless

J.B.'s attitude changed quickly, so he must have seen the immediate change in his mother's peace of mind. Before long, he told my friend, Joy Hill, "That is the best thing my mother has ever done for herself!"

I told J.B. and Lorna that I would find a job with a different pace and different responsibility after I was rested. My children knew that I never lacked for things to do. With a four-bedroom house, a large yard and all of my interests, I keep busy all of the time. They may have been thinking of my income.

I knew the minute I made the decision, my spending habits would have to change drastically. Making the decision was the hard part for me, living with my decision is easy. My freedom and peace of mind provides most of my needs at this point in life.

Living in the country now is different than when I was a child on the farm. I have all of the modern conveniences and comforts of life. When my husband was alive, we had a working farm, and did we work! After his death, many changes had to be made for me to continue living here. After Lorna got married and J.B. left for college, many more changes had to be made so I could live here alone and be efficient.

I have always been a very independent person, so it was important for me to continue to be so and feel like the farm was not falling into ruins. All of the livestock were sold and the farm ground was sown to brome grass. The pasture and brome were rented by the year to a neighbor. I then became a "patio farmer," sitting on the patio and waiting for the yearly income.

It was not quite that easy, as there were ditches to fill and erosion to stop. To say nothing of cutting brush and controlling excessive vegetation, especially musk thistle. This farm had more than enough work for a couple with two kids, let alone just a widow. With all of the needed changes, most things were never done the same with the main farmer gone.

With changes comes growth, and I had to learn how to grow alone. It was very difficult at first, but time and effort helped me to grow and become satisfied. When Loren died, my co-workers thought I would sell the farm and move to the city. To ease their minds I would tell them, "I make my money in town, but I live in the country. I won't leave the farm unless the banker gets cranky!"

Leaving hospital duty and returning my full attention to my property in the country was a good choice for me. My friends were elated to see that I had regained my humor and that, once again, I was fully enjoying myself.

19

"GET OUT OF MY GARDEN!" I yelled to a drunken Indian man as he lay there with his cowboy hat at his side and his cowboy boots, one off and one on.

What a sight to see! I live on a farm in the Kansas Flint Hills and cowboys are seen regularly, but not lying drunk in my garden.

Being a nurse, dealing with a drunk is not unusual for me. Dealing with cowboys in the Flint Hills was not unusual either. I could easily see that dealing with a drunken cowboy with one boot off, lying in my garden, was going to be a big problem.

I live on Highway #31, and my garden is out by the road. I have lots of friends, and I quickly knew they would love to see this episode from a distance so they could tease me about it for years to come. I can take ribbing as well as giving it to others, but I chose not to leave this drunk in my garden, so I got him on his feet and on his way.

This man had always admired my garden from the highway and would stop from time to time to beg garden goodies. I have always shared my vegetables but tried to avoid him as he was always under the influence. My husband, Loren, was not at home at the time, so I told the guy the onions were not ready to pull. He proceeded to walk out in the garden and check the onions for himself. For whatever the reason, he laid down, took off one boot, and his hat fell off and there he laid!

My first thought was to yell at him and get him on his feet, with or without his boots and hat. With my insistence, he got up and carried one boot out of the garden, but he left his hat there!

I quickly retrieved his hat and encouraged him to take it and leave. He left without his hat, and I doubt if he ever knew where he left it and why. I sure couldn't tell you why he left his hat!

Thank God, no one drove by while I got him to his feet and out of my hair. I had to make a quick choice as to how I was going to handle that problem. I sighed as I saw him head west.

I was relieved that my choice to yell at him and that my tough approach with the size of my God-given body was enough to make him listen and move on. God only knows what I would have done next. In that instance, I would have had another chance, but so often in life our first choice is our only chance.

At that point in my life, my sense of humor was intact, but dealing with drunks was not my favorite thing to do. I do not understand why anyone chooses to allow drugs of any kind to rule his or her life. In my own mind, I feel that each and every one of us makes a decision when we choose to avoid drugs or to use them. Once a person becomes dependent upon a drug (yes, alcohol is a drug), life is tough for them, and they make people around them suffer because of their dependency. So many people fail to recognize that one beer contains one shot of alcohol, the same as drinking whiskey and dependency is possible.

We have to want to be drug free, to be in charge of our mind and body, in order to live life to the fullest and to have freedom. I have never wanted anyone or anything to be in charge of my body and soul.

I was born free, and freedom has been my choice. Being born in the country and living most of my life on a farm allows me to be out with nature and feel free. Breathing good clean air and working in the soil is good for my soul; it is all the "kick" I need on life. Nature is a "real high" for me.

When I entered a Catholic School of Nursing, I was informed that over-indulgence of alcohol could be cause for immediate dismissal. To quote the nun, "If you get drunk, we will not only tell you to leave, we will help you pack!" That was the second reason I had for not getting drunk by experimenting with too much alcohol. The nuns quickly reconfirmed my first reason, not to let alcohol make my decisions.

While on affiliation for pediatric training, we heard quite a different speech about indulging in alcohol, "If you get drunk, use the elevator and clean up your own mess!" The administration at the hospital school was very lenient with the rules of alcohol, but was very strict about student nurses not fraternizing with the medical interns.

Several of the student nurses went out for the evening, and some of the medial interns showed up at the same place. One nurse got drunk enough that she could not walk alone, so one of the interns was helping me walk her to the nurse's quarters. Another student, Kathy, who was "real happy," decided to pick a flower from the housemother's flower bed. Kathy's snide remark, "I have been wanting to pick this flower for a long time!" brought the housemother to her feet and outside yelling, "Leave those flowers alone!"

When the intern saw the housemother, he let go of the drunken girl, and I could not hold her up alone. You guessed it, she fell into the flower bed digging with all fours!

That calamity upset the administration, so all of our home schools were notified. My home school was just a few miles across the river, but it was a "lo-o-o-o-ng" bus ride thinking about the possible outcome of my mistake. My parents' philosophy was fresh in my mind, "You get in trouble in school and you will be in bigger trouble at home!"

Upon my arrival at my home school, the nun said, "Sit down! Now, tell me one thing. Were you drunk or were you acting like you do here when we have a party?" I quickly replied, "Sister, I had a drink but I was not drunk!" She jumped to her feet and responded, "You get back over there, and I do not want to hear another word about you!"

I never knew what, if anything, happened to the drunken girl who fell into the flower garden when she was reported to her home school. I wonder if she has an alcohol problem today. I do not know as our careers never crossed paths again.

I thanked God that I had chosen not to get drunk and that I was not kicked out of nursing as my parents would have been unhappy with me but, most of all, I would have been devastated.

I went to school to train to be a nurse so I could become independent and have security. Too much alcohol would have destroyed me quickly. I never forgot that experience and never looked for entertainment with the use of alcohol or other drugs. I never missed any social function, but I was always in control of my behavior.

Forty years later I cannot help wondering about the use of alcohol and the philosophy of the affiliating school! What impact has their philosophy, "Use the elevator and clean up your own mess!" had in society. We know a lot more about addictions today, but quite possibly my home school philosophy saved this nurse from alcohol addiction.

20

EACH CHOICE THAT WE MAKE throughout life can make a big difference in the rest of our life and in the lives of our family or other people. Sometimes poor judgment in our choices results in mistakes that can never be corrected, no matter how hard we want to correct our mistakes.

As a nurse, I tried to teach that most mistakes are correctable if we readily admit our mistakes. For instance, when giving medications, if a mistake is made, if recognized and admitted, corrective action can be taken. Denial of our errors can be fatal, God forbid! Honesty is a goal for me, and I have admired that trait in my coworkers and staff members.

As a mother, I have tried to teach my children that not all mistakes are correctable, so extreme care needs to be taken in making choices. Sometimes we do not have a second chance to accomplish our goal.

My children were teenagers when Loren was killed in a car-tractor accident on the highway close to our home. The car hit the tractor, causing the tractor to flip and roll over Loren.

The young man who was driving the car will never be able to correct his driving mistake. All the grief, tears and prayers will not correct the error. I think my children, at that time, understood what I had been teaching them about decisions, choices and mistakes.

During our grieving period, I tried to impress upon my

children, Lorna and J.B., that when we choose to drive, we are risking our lives and the lives of others in case of an accident.

I chose to forgive the young man and not to destroy myself by hating an individual for the misfortune. Hatred would only eat away at me. I ask my children to consider the same option. We had no choice in Loren's death, but we did have a choice in the way that we accepted the loss.

Hate, envy or jealously are wasted emotions! So much time and effort can be used for the wrong emotion, and I choose to avoid wasting time and energy with those emotions.

I loved my husband, Loren, with all of my heart, but knew that accidents happen and nothing would bring Loren back. So the children and I had to go on living and finding our way without his direct help. Now he is our Guardian Angel. I thank him every day for his direction from above.

From every loss new strengths are developed, but it takes quite awhile to see life in that vein. We never know what we will have to endure next and to what depths of our soul we will have to search for the solution.

Very little can be done after a mistake is made that causes an untimely death. The person causing the death has to live with his mistake and go on with his life. I am quite sure it is very difficult! Time will ease his pain and make his life easier, and surely he will learn from his mistake. But what a sad way to learn that lesson in life!

As for the survivors of the person who was killed, time gives back to us what we lost, in wisdom, increased awareness of others' needs and memories of our dear Loren. Our wisdom should help us to avoid poor choices, thus preventing mistakes.

21

IN THE AGING PROCESS we do not have a choice in having aches and pains, but we do have a choice in how react to those aches and pains.

After many years of "nursing on roller skates," my aches and pains consumed my sense of humor. Nursing is hard work and a very demanding profession. With my personality of going faster and faster to get the assigned work done in the allotted time frame, I felt like I was on roller skates.

I am a very self-driven person and determined to get the work done. Maybe my dad, Fred Eastman, helped to instill that quality in me!

One day I was walking out through the pasture ahead of my Dad and he tapped me on the back of the legs, thus startling me, and I turned around and asked, "Why did you do that?" He replied, "You were walking too slow!" I have always given my dad the credit for putting spring in my step!

However, that personal trait and my goal put my body and mind at risk. My choice to walk fast when I was young was fine, but I failed to slow my pace to meet my body needs in my aging process. I can see now that I made the wrong choice as far as my body was concerned, but I could not walk away from a sick person who needed my care. Total dedication to the patient without putting my personal needs in order more than likely caused me and many of my professional friends to "wear out" before our time.

By the time I realized that I had lost my sense of humor at work and what the extra stress to my body was doing, I hurt so bad that I needed care for myself. I spoke to my physician, and he agreed that a few days of rest would be appropriate. But my supervisor at the federal hospital denied my request for sick leave with a doctor's slip. Remember, I worked the night shift and other nurses hated to relieve on that shift!

My joint pain was so severe in my left hip that I had to struggle to keep going to work night after night. Is it any wonder why my Guardian Angel, Loren, came to my rescue and saved me?

The choice to keep smiling through pain is very difficult, and I guess that is why my sense of humor failed me at that point in my life. I thank God and Loren for the help. I shudder to think what could have happened to me and my patients if I had ignored the message from above.

My family humor kept me in stitches when off duty, and my patients' cute little sayings kept me going while on duty for many years.

My sense of humor is what carried me through many problems in life, and it helped many of my family, friends and patients over the years. I am so thankful that my good sense of humor returned after a much needed rest and change of pace.

I was late in changing my pace, but at least with help I saw the light and had the will to change. I plan to remain in this pace or slower for the rest of my life. The aches and pain have not been cured, but they are better managed at this pace. I chose not to take a handful of pills every six hours for the rest of my life. Besides, medication always comes with side effects, and my theory is: You might as well deal with the pain where it is, as pain medicine in time will cause pain in the intestinal tract and possibly cause bleeding which causes more pain.

Time is a great healer, but we have to stop and take

time to "smell the roses"! For whatever the reason, I went everywhere on and off duty on a dead run. I was over thirty-five years old before I looked up or down for any length of time. I do not know where I was going at such a fast pace or what I thought I was going to do when I got there!

My father-in-law, Bryan Masters, said many times, "Do you think you are going to get all of the work done on this earth before you die?" My reply was, "No, but I am going to hang out this load of wash before we leave!"

I now sit and watch the sunrise and sunset as often as I like and enjoy each one immensely. Each one is different and a breathtaking sight to behold. I suggest you take time when you are young, and just maybe you will remain younger for a longer period of time.

My father-in-law was right; that batch of clothing would have waited! My only regret with raising our children: I should have cooked fewer big meals and made more bologna sandwiches on the way to the zoo. I could have learned to make the sandwiches in the back seat of the car on the way just as I did for the sport activities when our kids were involved. I packed sandwich meat in the cooler and took it to work. After work, Loren would drive us to the game while I made the sandwiches for the team when it was our turn to take supper for the team after the games.

Loren's sense of humor carried me over the rough road. He would tease me by saying, "Mrs. So and So could have made the sandwiches, but she had to work today!" He always knew how to get the best performance out of me.

22

"I JUST TURNED IN my two-week notice as I am resigning!" I related to my good friend and mentor, Bette Watson, R.N. She responded, "Then I will write out my resignation if you are going to leave this hospital! I have been wanting to quit and stay home with my son, Mike." I was very surprised and replied, "Don't quit just because I am leaving. You were here and had been for several years before I came!" She assured me, "You just gave me the courage that I needed. Now they can orient two new nurses for this ward."

I did not share with her or anyone why I was changing jobs after two short years into my professional nursing career. I wanted to get some emergency room experience as a registered nurse. But my big reason for changing jobs was to challenge Loren B. Masters with some serious thoughts for our future.

Loren and I started dating while we were working on the same geriatric, psychiatric ward with Bette and several other nurses playing cupid. Dating Loren, who was a psychiatric aide, while I was a registered nurse working on the same ward was unethical by the standards of the 1950s. Besides the professional standpoint, a man does not like the lady in the relationship to be the "boss."

One year after I changed jobs, I became the new bride of Loren B. Masters instead of his supervisor. He was less intimidated as an aide when I was a registered nurse in a different hospital.

There was a large salary decrease when I changed jobs. I knew money was an element of life, but not the goal for me. The new position was at a railroad hospital, where I joined a staff of great people with a family attitude, good personal values, and who were very dedicated to their patients. I loved that job better than other place of employment during my career.

The railroad hospital staff carried their good family values over into their nursing practice, and I could see how all of the patients benefited from that attitude. With my patients, I was trained to keep a professional distance, but the small mixture of family values added to the contentment of the patients.

I have always had a good nurse-patient relationship, and the respect for the patients was my reason to do the nursing care correctly. Patients deserve good treatment and a caring nurse. That is what made it impossible for me to leave patients' needs unmet regardless of time or my own body fatigue.

I am grateful that I learned early in my career that satisfaction is more important than money. I have always felt sorry for people who think money is the most important thing in life. I have seen money values cause many people misery. You can buy a lot of things with money, but you cannot buy health and happiness. My happiness and health are the two most important things to me.

Staying with a job that makes you unhappy is the worst thing a person can do in my opinion, regardless of salary, as life is a choice.

I did not change jobs often during my nursing career, but resigning from the same veteran's hospital at the start of my professional career and again near the end of my working years were two very good choices for me. Making good personal choices without closing the door to opportunity makes for a happy life.

The last resignation opened the door to accepting a part-time job as a registered nurse in a public school system. The part-time work was beneficial for me to survive until retirement wages would be available. The opportunity to work with young children was a pleasant change from working with older and critically ill patients. The pace was extremely different, and there was no comparison in the amount or kind of responsibilities. The hours of duty were during the daytime with all weekends off, which was entirely new for me. Time to rest and enjoy life between assignments restored my humor and outlook on life.

My school nursing supervisor introduced me to the other school nurses, "I want you to welcome our new substitute nurse, Dorothy Masters, to our district. We are going to retread her to think young." And they did!

The biggest responsibility of a school nurse is to be prepared to handle injuries resulting from anger and school violence, which is a big enough job in itself. That takes a much different approach than hospital nursing, especially critical care.

As a school nurse, the majority of your time and expertise is necessary for administration of medications. The children with Attention Deficit Disorder require a unique approach because of their anger and hyperactivity. The structure in society has become so lax that excessive anger has developed, requiring an entirely different nursing technique. When I first started in nursing, the patient would do exactly as you instructed, but that is not true in today's society.

Today's patients question everything that you try to do for them, and some rebel against everything. Many children with Attention Deficit Disorder rebel against every suggestion.

My part-time nursing schedule allows me to write and express myself and share my experiences with others. The return to freedom in the country without having to drive to the city every day was my biggest reward.

I had gone to school to train to be a nurse as I knew I

had to have security and be independent, which I needed again after Loren's death. I loved nursing as a way to earn an adequate living but enjoyed my work on the farm for a healthy, comfortable life style. I was fortunate to have fallen in love with a farmer who gave me back my country life style. The work was hard, but the rewards were many.

I guess it was natural for me to retreat to nature for my peace of mind after stressful nursing and trials of life caused my weariness. After quitting hospital work and regaining my peace of mind, my sense of humor returned fully. Within a few months I again felt free. My friend, Carol Weekes Swenson, who resides in California, could tell by my voice over the phone and on cassette tapes that my true humor and personality were returning. She once again could feel my happiness in my tone of voice.

Carol's opinion is very important to me, as we have been good friends since we attended the fourth grade together in grammar school. She and her family's close relationship were very beneficial to my healing process when I lost Loren and throughout the good times and bad times in my life. A close friend like her is better than any psychiatrist that money can buy.

I am fortunate to have fellowship with many good honest friends. In our small community of Harveyville, Kansas, I could name person after person who has made a difference in my life.

Another friend, Mary Lou Riat Anderson, had been a great help to me since we were in nurse's training together. She had been very concerned about me and my physical and mental health for quite some time before I resigned from floor duty. She was as relieved as many of my relatives were when she heard I had resigned to let my mind and body rest. She was well aware of my body discomfort and my need to let my life flourish back in to the bouncy, happy person that I used to be. Before long, she commented about the spring back in my step and the gleam in my eye.

23

"WHEN I WRAPPED MY TONGUE around that sugar, I couldn't stop eating the chocolate chip cookies that I made for my family!" remarked my friend, Aletta Akers Burgess.

I have known Aletta since school days but never as close friends until we worked together at the same nursing home. She had heard me tell patients and other staff how difficult a strict calorie reduction diet is to follow all of the time. She knew my theory on restricted diets and the down falls of diets. She recently gained some weight as most people do after reaching middle age. She had heard me counsel people against unsafe diet practices and encourage good health habits with proper nutrition.

I have always been overweight by most standards and all of the normal weight charts. Now Aletta tried to impress upon me that her spinach diet was doing real good for her and her friends here at work! She shared with me, "We easily lost our extra weight, and you could do the same thing if you follow our plan!" I stated, "Life is a choice and I will speak to you in a week or so. Meanwhile, I will continue to follow my plan of good healthy food in moderation or at least as moderate as possible as I exercise daily, and whatever will be!"

Aletta and her friends continued the week eating only spinach for lunch and talking about how easy their diet was to follow. I said, "Last night, I ate the refrigerator, just thinking about your diet!" I had not overeaten the night before, but I had been on lots of fad diets in my day and learned the hard way that they were headed for a binge and it was just a matter of time.

After Aletta admitted that she binged on the cookies, I never heard one more thing about an "easy spinach diet." I knew from my own experiences that fad diets do not work long, as they are too restrictive and do not provide adequate nutrition, so they leave the body screaming for calories of any kind, usually something sweet like home-made chocolate chip cookies.

The body and mind take over and eats as if they have been starved. Severe restricted diets cause the body and mind to feel starved, and out-of-control eating develops, and the recently lost weight comes back with extra pounds to "boot!"

I would love to be smaller and not gain weight so easily, but I am unable to change that fact. The years, through trial and error, plus experiences, have proved to me that size is less important than health and well-being. I chose to be active, thus being healthy, and control my weight as best that I can with a healthy eating plan and regular exercise.

I counsel young people that it is better to be fat than dead. Many of the severe methods of weight loss are killing people. With young girls especially, there is such a strong desire to be thin and beautiful at all costs, even death.

Life has many hard choices. I love life and I love people, and eating comes into play with nearly every social function. Many affairs do not offer low fat and low calorie choices in the food feast. Staying with low fat and low calorie treats is hard when your peers can indulge without excessive weight gain. Much persuasion is used to get people to try and enjoy all of the treats, causing harder choices for people with weight problems or those who are trying to avoid health problems.

Life is a choice, but it is very difficult to make the right choice when people around you are eating what you would like to eat instead of eating what is good for one's health. The best we can do is to live as healthy as possible with good food most of the time and good daily exercises for life.

I like to share with others what many people over the years have taught me, "It is what's inside that counts, not how the package is wrapped!" I have bought the philosophy, "You must love yourself if you want others to love you!" I have grown to love and appreciate my body, as it has served me well for a lot of years. God did not intend all of us to be fashion models. I would die before I reduced enough to be one! God built me for work and I have done that, so I feel good about my body and myself.

I have always lived in the country except for a few miserable years in the city getting my nursing education and starting my career. Living in the city was very restrictive for my needs for fresh air and freedom to roam. I have worked in the dirt and around farming duties most of my life, so one would think the shape of my body would be good. Wrong! As I have told my children many times as I am dragging a water hose around the yard or handling baled hay, "This is what keeps my arms so pretty!" Then I jiggle the loose, fatty skin on the bottom of my arm tissue and say, "I am not going back to lifting bales daily to get this muscle back up to the top of my arm where it belongs!" Humor is my only defense as crying does not help.

I had to learn to appreciate my body structure, as I started my life wishing for a small, pretty body, but it never happened. With the maturing process I learned to accept my structure as it got me where I wanted to go, and I could work as hard as I wanted and remain healthy. Health and happiness are the important things in life, not the size or shape of one's body!

24

I REGARD LIFE as being divided into three phases. The first phase is the birthing phase, and it is planned by our parents and made possible by God. We have no say or choice in our birthing phase. We do not get to select the method of our birth. We do not get to choose our parents.

The second phase is our living phase, and during this phase we have many, many choices. This is the period that we can make a difference in our life. The choice is ours and so is the responsibility.

The dying phase is planned by God. but if we do not make good choices as to how we live our life in the living phase, our death can be earlier and more severe.

Some people give very little planning to their living phase. They appear to give very little thought to their health, happiness or future. They tend to live and take things as they come without thinking of the possible consequences. When their untimely death is evident, they become angry and tend to place blame onto other people such as the medical community, their family or elements around them.

While working in the nursing profession, I have seen many angry people as they enter the final phase of life, the dying phase. I think most of the them are really angry with themselves but extend the anger to others in self-defense.

I truly feel if more people could be educated to give more thought and energy to their life in the living phase, the dying phase would be more tolerable. We can change our lives greatly during the living phase, but little can be done when death is evident. Our death can be aggravated by making poor choices during the living phase.

We have many ways to change our lives; our choices can enrich the way we live and improve the way we feel about ourselves and the world around us. One of the best ways to enrich our lives is to avoid over-self-indulgences. Over-indulgence of food is very unhealthy and can cause illness and an early death. Abuse of alcohol and drugs, both prescribed and illegal, does the body harm. Nicotine is a sure killer for the actual smoker and very dangerous to all who have to endure second hand smoke. Smokeless tobacco is very caustic to the user.

Lack of proper exercise promotes poor body function, and the chance for illness increases. When the chances of illness increase, the opportunity for a long, happy, healthy life decrease.

Good health habits are difficult to adopt and maintain but easy to drop, whereas poor health habits are easy to develop and very difficult to stop. Eating more than one really needs, no matter how good the food is, is a perfect example.

Eating too much good food has always been my passion! Doctor Fred looked over his glasses (this was before half-glasses), stared at me as a young nurse and said, "Dorothy, as you get older your weight will be harder to control!" Truer words were never spoken!

"At this time in my life, I have some areas that I label as "menopause sags." After all, time and gravity does not lift the tissue! But I feel we have to work towards a healthy body and a happy mind and then accept our size. Weight control is more difficult for some people, regardless of their age.

Another choice during the living stage is that sometimes people become too busy to enjoy all of their family throughout life. It appears to be easy for some folks to give lots of attention to their family and friends when babies are born and when deaths occur, but they have very little time to show attention during the living phase. They claim lack of time as an element for showing little interest. Many of them then have guilt feelings when dealing with deaths and thus are unable to accept death as a part of life.

We are born to die, and dying is the end result of living. I feel we should put most of our time, energy and love into the living phase. "Life is a game with no instructions!" The author is unknown, but the phrase is good food for thought. We must experiment as we live and gain knowledge. Living life is like taking a daily test. When we live a good life and be good to ourselves and our family and friends, God will take care of the rest.

The dying phrase is planned by God, as we all are on loan from God just for a little while. I can easily accept death if the dying person has lived and not just existed. I do not think God expected us just to exist.

My husband, Loren, had lived a good life and had helped many people in many different ways. He definitely left his mark in society, and that made it easier for me to accept his death, even with it being so untimely. I feel sorry for myself and his children and all of our family and friends because we miss his company so very much.

After many years of nursing dying people and watching my family and friends die, I developed my theory of death and dying, "The Rose Bush Theory."

This theory was a collection of thoughts and memories of lost loved ones collected while I sat by a rose bush as my favorite, beloved brother, Bob Eastman, died. The dew on the beautiful pink rose brought me closer to God as I accepted Bob's death and others.

"THE ROSE BUSH THEORY"

I relate life and death to a big, beautiful rose bush. Picture a large blooming rose bush and you can see your family or circle of friends. Some of the roses are in full bloom with gorgeous color and perfect shapes. Some roses are starting to form buds. Some of the buds never complete the full growing process. Some of the roses are dead and remain on the bush, while others are starting to wither.

Now relate each and every one of those blooms to different members of your family or your circle of friends, and you can see the living and dying process. Life is a process with death being the final phase. Please do not wait; live life to the fullest each and every day.

Keep in mind, to maintain that "rose bush" (loved ones) big and pretty, it must be fed, watered, nurtured, pruned, protected from the elements and loved with a gentle caress plus some tender talk. The care is more essential when caring for people.

My attitude and acceptance have not been easily developed! Now I accept death much easier than I did as a young person. When my father, Fred Eastman, died, I cried every time I was alone for many weeks. I continued my daily duties as a student nurse and lived my personal life, but I missed him so much. In fact, I still miss him, and I wish he could have known my husband and children.

The death of my mother, Golden Eastman, was also very difficult for me and my family, as my children were young, and with busy jobs and family duties there was little time for proper mourning. Grieving and the time to do so is a very important part of healing from the death of a loved one.

When I lost Loren, I thought I would die! Death is So-o-o-o-o Final — that it is hard to accept. There is always unfinished business. With the farm, two teenagers and a full time job, there was not sufficient time for proper grieving. Things had to be done, and they had to be done now! Again, I cried every day for months when I was alone. I carried on with my job and life with a stiff upper lip but fooled no one!

Before losing Loren, I had endured the death of my dad, mother, a sister, niece, plus a nephew and niece on Loren's side of the family. I guess you might say I have experienced death one way or another nearly every day of my adult life.

A very few years later, my brother, Clifford, died after many years of severe lung illness. All of the deaths were tough for me and my children. God helped me find a way and gave me time to say good-bye to my beloved brother, Bob. By the time my sister, Bessie, died, grieving was almost a process for me. There again, she had been ill with lung disease for years, and living was difficult for her. I must give Loren, my Guardian Angel, the credit for easing my pain and difficulty during my mourning period for Bessie, as he had provided me three months of rest between the busy hospital life and the time of her death. I must say he saved my life one more time, as this was the first family death I had endured without busy hospital duties.

Life is a process and we have to live a long time to figure out the best way to accomplish the process and ease all of our feelings into the proper spot at the right time. Coping is a good word, but it does not just happen. Learning to cope with loss is a real art, and it is different for everyone.

Now I know I healed from my husband's death as I watched my brother, Bob, die by inches. Having time to say good-bye and to relive our childhood memories together helped me to heal from the loss of my husband. Bob also loved my husband, Loren, only he called him "Mac." Loren thought Bob was the greatest, and we had a great time together through the years.

In the case of someone else's death, we do not have a choice, but we do have a choice in how we accept the death.

25

" I DO NOT WANT TO BREATHE this land one acre at a time through a respirator should I become terminally ill for any reason!" was my statement to J.B. and Lorna. My children were young when Loren was killed, but I had to depend on them, regardless of their young age, to carry out my wishes should I become terminally ill. I had to use communications that were understandable to young minds. We had bought the land for us and to be handed down to our family, so I did not want to breathe away the acres with mechanical devices. I do not see that as quality of life!

Each person has to make his or her own decisions about their life. With chronic lung disease very prevalent in my family, I definitely do not wish to prolong my natural life by the use of a respirator. I, for one, do not want to live an extended time by heroic measures or mechanical devices; therefore, I have signed a Living Will and keep it current. Each state and area have different rules and regulations, so I will not speak about the Living Will, except to say that everyone needs one. Please do not put off making it for another day. Life is short, but misery can go on indefinitely!

I will encourage each and every one of you to research the rules and regulations of Living Wills in your area and decide for yourself exactly what, if any, you want done for yourself. Do not leave the decision for your loved ones.

I have made my desires known to my children and medical contacts. I remind my children and update the Living

Will on a yearly basis. The responsible person in your life has to be strong and very persistent to make sure the medical community carries out the stated wishes in your Living Will.

Quality of life is important to me, not just quantity of life. In my nursing practice, I have witnessed too much quantity without quality! It was easy for me to make the decision to sign a Living Will.

Every individual has the right to leave written instructions as to how they want their final wishes to be carried out should the occasion arise at the time of their death.

Many people do not understand to what extremes the medical staff go in the event of prolonging life. Prolonging life at all cost does not appeal to me at this time in my life. I have lived a good life, and extra years attached to a machine is not my idea of quality of life. Once someone is put on the machines, getting the machines turned off can be very tricky and sometimes impossible!

I do not wish to leave excessive medical bills for someone else to pay. I like life with quality to be prolonged, but I hate to witness the prolonging of death, and that is what happens in medical institutions without the proper written instructions of your wishes.

Communication is necessary between family members so they can carry out the desires of the person who is dying. Many people are unable to speak of their upcoming death. Others want to talk about death and are not allowed to speak, as the person to whom they are speaking is unable to accept death, let alone speak of death.

It has been my experience that many people do not think about their destiny until it is upon them. After their health starts to decline, then they try to make big changes and sometimes begin to search for solutions to their failing health, many of which are inappropriate.

Many times new organs are transplanted and the patient did not change their lifestyle and all is lost, but the medical bills keep adding interest for all of us to pay one way or another.

Sometimes the person does not have the knowledge or resources to evaluate the problems of his lifestyle. On the other hand, many people disregard advice and continue poor health habits and develop a severe illness.

Smoking habits with the related health problems are a good example. In the last several decades, I have seen severe illnesses from nicotine and excessive health care dollars spent on patients who had been advised to stop smoking years ago. On a national level, we hear of ways to control health care expense, but the simple advice is ignored until severe problems develop.

For example, after all that has been done, smoking is on the rise, especially among teenagers. Drinking alcohol is so prevalent in the colleges, especially at the fraternities and sororities. Our approach is not working on drug abuse, and the education has not been the key as we felt it would be several years ago.

Excessive health care costs continue to soar until all of our health care insurance is at risk, as no one can pay the outlandish medical bills.

Often I hear, "You cannot put a price on a human life," which is true. But, by the same token, one person, one state or one nation cannot spend money they do not have. Or at least, they cannot spend it for long! This may explain the dilemma that our nation is experiencing with health care costs and the solutions.

I feel my last professional mission is to teach people to prevent disease by managing their health to the best of their ability with conservative medical intervention and accept the outcome. Do not wait for the medical community to save your life after you have ignored preventive illness information.

My idea is to live well, manage my health and to die with dignity. I pray with all of my heart that I will drop dead while tending my rose bushes, but I am in no hurry.

26

"LOREN HAS BEEN IN AN ACCIDENT and we need to know what to do for him until the ambulance arrives?" was the message I received from Nellie, my sister-in-law, while I was at work.

My heart stood still, but my professional being said, "Keep him warm and do not move him until the ambulance arrives!"

As I headed toward the local hospital, I prayed, as I felt Loren had a broken neck from the description given to me by Nellie, as he had been thrown from the tractor.

When I arrived at the Emergency Exit, our local ambulance had just arrived. I thought, "My, they were fast! They had to drive 30 miles and I only had to drive across town!"

I parked my car and ran to the ambulance, when the E.M.T.'s opened the door and I saw a little old woman on the cot and shrieked, "Oh, no!" The attendants asked me what was the matter?

I managed to say, "I'll tell you later!"

I knew there was a big problem as our area only had one ambulance service.

When the E.M.T.'s returned, I told them, "Loren has been in an accident and I thought he was on the cot!"

They asked a few questions and left, so I knew they drove out to make radio contact and find out what they were to do. They drove back in the lot immediately, so I knew that Loren was coming by another service.

I chose to wait out in the area of the ambulance drive so I could see Loren the minute he arrived. I knew from experience, the emergency staff would hide me out in a room and I would be unable to see Loren when he arrived. I can deal with the facts, but not knowing bothers me a lot.

"Oh, No-o-o-o," I muttered to myself when I saw my husband dead on the ambulance cot as he was brought into the hospital. I knew our lives would never be the same, but life goes on, as it should.

Accepting the death of loved ones is not easy, but you have no choice! You have a choice in living, to live as you like, time permitting. With death, there is no choice.

Accepting the death of your beloved husband is the most difficult thing you will ever endure, but you have no choice. Death is so final and you can never visit with the person again. You can talk to the dead person, but you usually are unable to hear a reply. The thing I miss most in the loss of my loved ones is the direct communication. Indirect communication does not offer an immediate response. The only time I heard Loren's voice since his death was the night I resigned.

I had to accept Loren's death and continue living for myself and our children. I was not in the accident. I had no control over the event or how it came to be, so I had no guilt feelings about Loren's death. Without guilt or blame, acceptance is easier.

I started losing loved ones at a very early age. By the time I had to deal with the loss of my husband, I had experienced loss many times. Loss is loss, but it affects you differently each time as you learn to cope with the losing of loved ones.

My dad, Fred Eastman, died of lung cancer while I was a student nurse and only nineteen years old. Being young and away from home made my mourning period even tougher. During that time my case study at the hospital was a man dying of lung cancer. It was hard for me to deal with dying both in family and my profession. Watching my patient die and thinking about my father was difficult.

My sister, Helen Hamilton, died at age forty-seven, when I was forty. It is scary to accept the death of a sibling who is close to your own age. You wonder if you will die soon! Helen's death made me more conscious about my health habits and my own mortality. My philosophy of living "the living phase" to the fullest started to develop at that time. Helen was a heavy smoker, and I felt it contributed to her death. Helen was also a diabetic at the time of her death, due to the excessive medical interventions with steroids.

The last time I saw Helen alive, she was sitting beside a big box of doughnuts, taking oxygen while smoking a cigarette. As a nurse, I have never forgotten that picture.

What is wrong with that picture? Someone had to bring her the cigarettes and doughnuts, as she was house-bound and physically unable to go out and buy her own. Why do we kill people with blind kindness, especially after they killed themselves with cigarettes or other vices?

Many people have died in my family from the ills of tobacco, and many of my family still smoke, Go figure! Life is a choice, but I cannot imagine why they want to suffer a slow death by gasping for air.

My mother, Golden Eastman, age 84, died one year after Helen's death. She had what is called a normal death after having a prior heart attack and stroke from which she recovered, but she had some emphysema from second-hand smoke. She died in a local nursing home where she lived.

I was the director of another nursing home in a neighboring town. Between caring for my young children, my husband and my professional duties which included twenty-four-hour call, I, again had very little time for proper mourning. With the pace of my life and the losses occurring around me, I began to think more about my own mortality. I was afraid the twenty-four-hour call, seven days a week, was putting my health at risk, so I went back to hospital floor duty six months before my husband was killed.

My brother, Clifford Eastman, died of lung disease after a long period of suffering. He stopped buying cigarettes long before his death, but he would smoke someone else's cigarette every now and then. He would cough and gasp for air while turning blue, and this went on for years. He used oxygen as he slept for years before his death.

I am very glad that I never developed the smoking habit, as it is must be very hard to shake. In my career I have seen patients smoke until the very end, regardless. I have talked to many people who have never been able to shake the habit but wished they could, whereas I have talked to others who say quitting was hard, but they did it!

My brother, Bob Eastman, died of lung cancer at age fifty-four. He was two and one-half years older than I. He, likewise, was a heavy smoker. Needless to say, I hate smoking or tobacco in any form. During his death, I developed my "Rose Bush Theory." I loved Bob with all of my heart, but I did not like the fact he chose to smoke himself into a early grave and leave me behind to live life without him.

I feel life is a choice, and a heavy smoker chooses to die early and usually has a traumatic death. I have heard lots of people respond to the medical opinion about the health risk from smoking, "I am going to die anyway; it might as well be from smoking!" My reply mentally or literally is, "But why do you wish to suffer so?"

While I watched Bob die for days, I would sit on the front porch just outside his window and gaze at the big beautiful rose bush. With the dew on the roses, I could relate to the religious aspect. With a variety of live and dead blooms, I could relate to life and death.

While my "Rose Bush Theory" was developing in my head, many of our family members sat in the kitchen, grieving and smoking. When they asked why I sat on the porch, I would reply, "Just thinking as I enjoy nature, breathing fresh air while I am close to Bob."

I was trying subconsciously to relay a message about choices in life, I assume now! At the time I was thinking about what Bob had told me many time, "I will smoke and drink booze until I die!" And he did, until he was unable to get the alcohol and to hold a cigarette. I recall saying to him on many occasions, "Life is a choice!" And the choice was his!

Bob and I were the closest in age, and we spent lots of time together working and playing while growing up. When he was taking radiation treatments and dying, we had hours together traveling to and from the hospital and at his home before his wife came from work. This time was spent reliving our childhood memories, and it was a wonderful way to say good-bye.

I did not have a chance to say good-bye to Loren, and this time with my favorite brother somehow helped me with the loss of both relationships.

The grieving and mourning process is different for everyone, but love from family members and friends is of the utmost importance.

By the time my sister, Bessie Eastman, and my brother, Jack Eastman, died, I had lots of experiences with losing loved ones. Death never gets easy for the ones left behind, but it does get easier to give them up. Both Bessie and Jack died of lung disease after many years of poor health. Now you know why I hate tobacco in any form, as I have my own lung difficulties from second-hand smoke.

I started losing my immediate family at the age of nineteen and have continued losing people close to me, making me feel older than my actual age.

Jack lived the longest of any of my siblings, and his lung disease was diagnosed first. He chose to deal with his symptoms immediately! He stopped smoking when he left the doctor's office. He walked and did other exercises and used oxygen for many years before his death. Life definitely has choices! Do you care to exercise your right to live?

Having been a nurse for all of my adult life, death has been around me constantly. I have learned to accept death, and that has taught me how to live. And to live life to the fullest. I have found through living, the best things in life are the simple things, many of which are free, like good clean, fresh air, wild flowers in the lush green grass and the birds of nature. I have little interest in complex living or expensive material things.

Losing loved ones and many wonderful patients, my interest in nature has increased, making it easier for me to relate to life and death situations.

Love is a choice and the biggest and most important choice of all.

You are free to love whomever you choose. However, they may not love you in return. But, the choice is still yours, as you can walk away and not look back, or you can continue loving them in your mind as you fill your life with other distractions or you can hold on which brings you nothing in the end.

Love is to be passed around, and this is not to be confused with sex. There are many ways to love another person. Love of mankind is not to be confused with passionate love.

Passionate true love happens, usually when you least expect it. And I am not going to dwell on that type of love as it happens and God is in charge of true love.

Love is the only thing you can give away and get back as much or more than you gave. The best example of that type of love is returned from your children, grandchildren or other small children. Every small token of love given to children comes back in large bills of genuine love.

My mother-in-law, Mae Masters, used to say about children, "It takes so little to please them!" Now that I am in the grandmother stage of life, I know what she meant. My grandchildren are pleased with every small token of my love. And so were our children, but sometimes I was too busy to notice, which was a mistake on my part. This is a life lesson that may be learned too late in life, so what I am saying is: Stop and smell the roses!

It is easy for me to give love and to receive love in return. It always amazes me when I tell someone I love them, meaning fellowship love, and they squirm and have difficulty in returning their love in any form. I think to myself, this person has a problem with any kind of love except romantic love. Isn't that a sad thing?

I found out at an early age, the more love you give the more you receive. As the words of a popular song state, "Love can build a bridge!"

I found the right partner in true love, but an accident took Loren away from me physically. But he is always with me spiritually. Today, May 21, 1999, would have been our thirty-ninth anniversary had he survived the accident. I still have our memories and our pictures together, so I feel I have everything. I talk about him and think about him on a nearly daily basis which makes some people uncomfortable.

Life brings about lots of changes, many of which we cannot change, but we can always choose how we react to the situation. The Serenity Prayer has helped me to adjust to many things in my life.

SERENITY PRAYER

"GOD grant me the SERENITY to accept the things I cannot change. COURAGE to change the things that should be changed, and the WISDOM to know the difference."

Unconditional love is hard to explain and hard as it must be learned first-handed. We sometimes think we love our family and nothing will change that, but life has a way of presenting problems that put our love to the test. My love for people has tested me many times, but I recently learned the true meaning of unconditional love. My definition of unconditional love: Love will remain intact for your loved ones, no matter what happens!

When our family crisis developed, I had to examine my love for my children and to what point I was willing to continue my loving relationship with my family. I chose unconditional love, and I am grateful that I was able to see life and our crisis in that manner.

When we witness other families in crisis, it is easy to decide what we would do in the same circumstances. The hard part comes when the crisis is in your family and the family togetherness is threatened. People without unconditional love will disown their family members when they do not follow the family trend.

Life brings a lot of changes; therefore, family units change and not always for the best. One must accept the things he or she is not able to change. You do not have to like the change in your family structure, but you must be willing to accept things as they become if you want to continue your happiness. I chose to adopt the Serenity Prayer.

The pursuit of happiness is the most important lifetime task. We must be allowed to pursue our own happiness. Our happiness is our own responsibility, not our spouse's. I made the big mistake of thinking that Loren was responsible for some of my happiness. After his death, I figured out it was totally my responsibility and always had been. Some things we learn by mistakes and by living in the real world.

We must not allow others to derail our pursuit for happiness, and by the same token we cannot wait for others to make us happy.

We all have the choice to be happy if we use our options. We have the option to walk away from unhappiness by choosing new friends and new interests. All of us will endure pain and suffering from time to time, and that's life! I have found that physical exercise and new interests have helped me through the rough times of life. I refuse to let my pain and suffering make me miserable.